PRESIDENTIAL
VISITS TO
NEW JERSEY

PRESIDENTIAL
VISITS TO
NEW JERSEY

★ ★ ★ ★ ★ A History ★ ★ ★ ★ ★

PETER ZABLOCKI

THE
History PRESS

Published by The History Press
Charleston, SC
www.historypress.com

First published 2022

Manufactured in the United States

ISBN 9781467153089

Library of Congress Control Number: 2022939480

For my dear friends Tom and Oliver.
—PZ

CONTENTS

PREFACE

The American presidency, the highest office a citizen of our county can hold, is essentially nothing but a job fulfilled by a specific—albeit not necessarily ordinary—American citizen. As with any job, there are particular responsibilities one has to meet, people they have to see and impress and things they have to do before they can take time to rest. Yet—and perhaps for a good reason—we are fascinated with the individuals who take up the mantle at any given time. It is ironic, especially considering that when our founding fathers set out to write the Constitution of the United States, Congress, not the president, was to be the primary representative of the American people—hence the article I designation. Part of the executive branch, one of the three branches that make up our national government, the president's job is to execute, or rather enforce, and carry out the laws passed by Congress in their plainest terms, nothing less and nothing more.

Around the early nineteenth century, a string of men viewed this job as requiring increased influence and even challenged the concept of a Congress superseding the president. Men such as Andrew Jackson, James K. Polk, William McKinley, Teddy Roosevelt and even Woodrow Wilson and Franklin D. Roosevelt challenged these established paradigms with strong personalities and forceful visions for the nation both domestically and abroad. During their presidencies, Congress would assume the role of a supporter—at least in the public's eyes—and not the intended leader the founding fathers intended it to be. According to historian Robert Dallek, in the case of the latter four presidencies, "It was a welcomed change from the stumbling administrations of the nameless, faceless presidents who occupied the White House for thirty-five years after Lincoln's assassination."[1]

All of a sudden, Americans saw forceful and charismatic national leaders governing more effectively than Congress and their state-selected representatives. The executive office and the man (they have only been men up to this point) who occupies it, became the object of people's admiration. In the plainest terms, the president became the nation's most watched, admired and simultaneously criticized individual. The men in power only fueled this assumption through their campaign promises, seemingly always providing ready-made solutions to issues that could not be corrected in a single term, a fix-all, great figure meant to be looked up to and respected, yet also blamed if need be. In a nation designed to reject any form of monarchy, the single person holding the executive office of the United States has come to embody the entire country—its fears and its hopes. Ironically, at least in relation to the Constitution's original intent, Americans do not always recall the names of all our state representatives and senators. Yet, we would be hard-pressed to forget the men whom we've called commander in chief.

Today, the American people refer to the president of the United States as the most powerful person in the world, which, considering the nation's military status, may not be too far from the truth. Yet, when looking at it from a strictly social perspective, the president is the ultimate celebrity to an average citizen. What he does, where he goes and what he says are all open to scrutiny, with hordes of magazines, blogs, vlogs and YouTube influencers waiting to pounce on every little imperfection or blunder. There is celebrity news, and then there is news about the president. This celebrity-like obsession or phenomenon has been around for decades; the only things that have changed are the means of communicating it to the public. Before the internet, newspapers, radio and television acted as the lens that fueled the spectacle; now, it is the combination of all of them. The chapters that follow attempt to re-create the feelings of awe and pride that often accompany the American president on his public appearances. This media frenzy arises each time the ultimate celebrity comes to town, whether it's for an official visit, to take a few days off work or to say a few words as an honorary guest speaker for a good cause—or, as was once the case, to die.

Now, while looking at New Jersey's electoral history of the past half century would have one dreaming blue, the reality is that the state's political paradigms have shifted quite often from Republican to Democrat, only to do it all over again. The state of New Jersey, one of the original thirteen colonies, has taken part in all presidential elections—fifty-nine to be precise.

President Warren G. Harding dedicating a monument in Princeton, New Jersey, in May 1922. *Joseph Bilby.*

And although it's one of the smaller states, its population density puts it just behind Rhode Island for having the most electoral votes per square mile. And since we are staying precise, New Jersey had fourteen electoral votes in 2022, a drop from seventeen just a half century prior. Thus, together with its packed electoral votes and traditionally fickle electorate, the Garden State found itself a vital state come November quite a few times in its history. And thus, it was graced quite often in its past with the most significant honor: a visit from the nation's biggest celebrity, the president of the United States.

The intent of this work is not to chronicle every time a president stopped by the state on his way to an important meeting in nearby New York or had to spend the night in a New Jersey hotel. What it does set out to do is highlight every notable appearance the American executive had in the small northern state, especially when appeasing New Jersians would have mattered in the upcoming election. This author dares to say that quite a few times, New Jersey was a battleground state, a state that mattered to the outcome of a national election. It most certainly counted in 1912, when the Garden State's sitting governor, Woodrow Wilson, decided to cut his governorship short and run for the presidency, even though his state favored the former president Theodore Roosevelt.

Its importance was also on full display when thousands of people came out to support the Democrat Franklin D. Roosevelt when he visited the state in 1936, and they proved their support at the polls four consecutive times. New Jersey switched allegiances when it hopped on the "I Like Ike" bandwagon in 1952. There was a general fear among Republicans that the state would revert to its Democratic sentiments of the prior decades. And although Ike secured New Jersey for two terms with many appearances in the state, his party lost to the flip-flopping nature of New Jersey in 1960, when a certain charming young Democrat came to town and promised the people a vision of a "new frontier." Still, the visit from who was probably the most glamorous president of all time surprisingly paled in comparison to that of his successor, Lyndon B. Johnson, who toured the state in 1964. After voting Republican for most of the two decades following Lyndon B. Johnson, New Jersey once again became a battle state in 1992, when H.W. Bush and Bill Clinton made it their prerogative to court its people through numerous appearances.

All of this is not to say that there were no lesser-known and shorter stays from American commanders in chief in the Garden State. And while those are worthy of acknowledgement, they simply did not elicit the same response as the more official visits discussed within these pages. New Jersey proved to be an excellent go-to for quick media appearances and speeches. These drummed up just enough of a media frenzy to keep the leaders and their parties relevant in nonelection years. In some cases, they even helped maintain their legacies after their times as president of the United States came to an end. After all, it was not every day that the most powerful person in the world stopped by one's state. There were multiple instances in which presidents swung by New Jersey to speak on a given cause, whether they were nationally focused topics, such as women's suffrage, which President Wilson discussed in 1912, or something as specific as talking to a union of steelworkers, which Nixon did in 1971. Perhaps not surprisingly, the state was also abuzz each time a former president stopped by for a media event—as was the case when Gerald Ford presented a Boy Scout award in 1983; George H.W. Bush spoke at the Summit of Volunteerism in 1997; and Harry S. Truman went to Bergen County to watch a theater performance by his daughter, an aspiring actress, in 1961. If the president—even a former one—was in town, it almost always made the front page.

Because a president's job does not end with winning elections and giving speeches, this book also highlights the notable moments when the head of state decided to drop into the Garden State to get some rest. Way before recent president Donald Trump took weeklong working vacations from his golf club at Bedminster, New Jersey, other commanders in chief sought out the benefits of resting at the Jersey shore. Noted presidents who graced the Jersey beaches include Franklin Pierce, James Buchanan, Andrew Johnson, Ulysses S. Grant, Rutherford B. Hayes, Chester A. Arthur, Benjamin Harrison, William McKinley and Woodrow Wilson. And no destination was more popular than Cape May's Congress Hall Hotel, which served as a "summer White House" for Benjamin Harrison and at least four other presidents on a less permanent basis. On the other hand, President Grant chose Long Branch as his permanent vacation spot, building a cottage (more like a seaside mansion by today's standards) where he would spend nearly the entirety of each summer throughout his two terms as president. And just as in the recent case of President Trump, the media was not always happy with the nation's leader taking time off to regenerate at the Jersey shore. A *New York Times* editorial from 1855 spent a decent amount of its print space complaining about President Pierce taking time off in New Jersey's Cape May when the nation was busy heading toward a Civil War.[2]

New Jersey was also the birthplace of one president and the permanent home of at least two others. Yet this occurred either before or after the individuals held the nation's highest office and thus only called for a mere mention instead of dedicated chapters. Although he did not spend much time in the Garden State, President Grover Cleveland was born in Caldwell in a home that remains a state historical site. A son of a Presbyterian minister who led the congregation next door to the modest home, Grover lived in

New Jersey until the age of four, when his father relocated to a church in upstate New York. The next American president to spend significant time in the state would be Woodrow Wilson, first as the president of Princeton University and later as the New Jersey governor. The first nonclergy president of the institution, Wilson moved to the state in 1890, when he became a Princeton professor of jurisprudence and political economy before being appointed the university's president in 1902, a post he held until running for and winning the governorship in 1910. He would remain in the state for two more years before launching his national political career by being elected to the office of the presidency in 1912, an election that made for a New Jersey spectacle with a former, current and future American president visiting the state within weeks of each other.

Another head of state—this time a former one—who called New Jersey home was none other than Richard Nixon. While his political career began in California, where his presidential library and home now stand, it was in the Garden State that he spent the last thirteen years of his life, often spotted around the town of Saddle River. Eventually, his ailing health would see him and his wife move to a nearby private community in Park Ridge, New Jersey. It was also not a coincidence that the said towns he chose to settle in were Republican strongholds. And while Richard Nixon would not pass away in New Jersey, instead taking his last breath at the New York–Presbyterian Hospital on April 22, 1994, that feat was already accomplished by another commander in chief, James A. Garfield. After being shot and all but killed by his doctors, who ignored new medical studies on bacteria and infections, the ailing president was moved to the resort town of Long Branch on the Atlantic coast in September 1881. The idea was that the cool New Jersey ocean breeze would help his quickly deteriorating health. It did not.

In the state's most recent history, two modern presidents visited to assess the damage caused by national disasters. First was President Barack Obama, who came to New Jersey in late October 2012 to witness firsthand the damage caused by Hurricane Sandy and pledge federal government assistance toward rebuilding. The event was mired in political controversy, as the conservative New Jersey governor Chris Christie was openly criticized by his constituents for catering to the Democratic national leader. The same treatment did not befall Christie's successor, Governor Phill Murphy, as he welcomed President Joe Biden to tour Hurricane Ida's damage in the Garden State in 2021. And although the men were here for sad reasons, their presence still solicited the media frenzy that so often accompanies a presidential visit to any given state.

It is easy to say that a lot has changed over the years regarding the growing nastiness of presidential campaigns and the all-too-often scrutiny that follows American presidents. Yet looking at history from the perspective of past eras—specifically by reading newspaper accounts and watching television news clips—it becomes evident that not much has changed at all. The main impetus of this book was to showcase through selected events the excitement and regional pride that accompanies presidential state visits—in this case, in New Jersey. We read and learn about these larger-than-life-itself individuals from our history books. They are pantheons, almost legends, who help us remember the significant historical events that shaped our nation—the wars, social movements, depressions, setbacks and accomplishments. In American minds, fueled by the media—whether through newspapers, the nightly news or the latest tweet—they become more than mere mortals. Hence, it is no surprise that any visit by a president, whether past, present or future, was and still is welcomed with pride.

Still, it would be tough to trace every time a former or soon-to-be American president visited a given state. In my hometown alone, there is circumstantial evidence that points to the fact at least five individuals who held or would hold the office visited the area at one point or another. There are times when these former leaders of the free world came to the Garden State to speak on behalf of other local politicians for thirty minutes and then left—something that has been a lot more popular of late. Other times, their stay did not exceed more than an hour, as with former president H.W. Bush landing a helicopter on a local soccer field to meet with his dying friend in a nearby hospital, a mere twenty-minute stay. There is also no mention of Herbert Hoover's quick drive through the state and an impromptu fishing outing that lasted a couple of hours. Brief visits such as these do not evoke the same feelings as official presidential visits—there is no spectacle associated with it, no event quite so worthy of front-page news. Plainly speaking, events such as these are too short and too unofficial to spend too much time discussing.

And thus, this collection looks at the times when an American president, the ultimate celebrity, came to visit New Jersey and made its people feel like—albeit for a brief moment—the national spotlight was on them. The hordes of people lining up on the streets, the media frenzy, the partisan commentary, it is all here to be relived once again, lest we forget that these larger-than-life figures walked among us, shook hands, spoke, campaigned, were born, lived and even died right here in the Garden State. This is not a book about politics or agendas, and it does not set out to favor one political party over the other. It is not necessarily a book about politics or political figures either. Instead, it is a story of specific events where the people of New Jersey came together to celebrate the democratic process and, if not for anything else, peek at the most potent national figure of their time.

Peter Zablocki

ACKNOWLEDGEMENTS

I would like to say a sincere thank-you to my wife for her constant support throughout this journey. Also, a big thank-you goes out to the people who took a chance on me when I first started writing: J. Banks Smither, Michael Dolan, Stephen Harding, Bill Hogan, and Susan Kilby—none of this would be possible without them. I am also grateful to those who are always there to lend an ear when I need to bounce some ideas off them: Dr. Steve Racine, Danielle Elia, Heather Pollak, Matt Arroyo, Katy Johnson, George Economou, Lori Vertucci, and Kevin Kane. Thank you to the countless librarians who have helped me over the years with all of my research, especially Ms. Laura Petersen, Ms. Jenny Sassaman, Ms. Maryellen Liddy, Ms. Illene Lefkowitz, Ms. Krystine Whitmore and Ms. Siobhan Koch.

1

LINCOLN'S PLEA FOR UNITY

There is no denying the fact that as far as national elections go, the election of 1860 is the most infamous of them all when examining the brief history of America. The issue of slavery had split the Democratic Party, turned the affair into a four-way race, and all but ensured the election of a Republican newcomer, Abraham Lincoln. Within mere days, the South Carolina legislature voted to secede from the Union, and lame duck president James Buchanan watched helplessly as the state's militia seized federal territories without any interference. As Lincoln awaited his inauguration on March 4, 1861, five additional states voted to leave the Union, forming the Confederate States of America. By the time the war began in the spring of 1861, five more states would join the original six; vote a U.S. senator from Mississippi, Jefferson Davies, as their president; and adopt a constitution that emphasized states' rights and the protection of slavery.

In the most precarious time for the president-elect, all Lincoln could do was strengthen his coalition and support from the northern people for the inevitable conflict looming on the horizon. He would need unequivocal support from the Union, specifically one state in the north that rebuffed the Republican candidate in the 1860 election. Abraham Lincoln needed to make a showing in New Jersey before taking up the mantle as the commander in chief—he needed to know if the Garden State he did not win a month prior would stand behind him in his hour of need. The ultimate test would come on February 21, 1861, as the tall, lanky president-elect stepped off the ferry in Jersey City to tour the Garden State.

The seeds of the Civil War and the overall distrust between the North and the South could probably be traced to the very beginning of the British colonization of North America. However, while the issue of slavery was often compromised on in Congress to preserve the political balance within the legislative branch, the social components of the issue could not be tucked away by legislation. With the rise of the abolitionist movement in the North, southern leaders saw the North's complacency with limiting the growth of the radical doctrine of complete emancipation of slavery as a threat to their slavery-based society. When former members of the Whig Party—many of whom had abolitionist tendencies and backgrounds in opposing the spread of slavery—met in 1854 to establish the Republican Party, southern newspapers almost instantly threatened secession if the new party was ever to come into power. By the election of 1860, the South's only hope of stopping the Republicans and their chosen candidate, Abraham Lincoln, lay in the Democratic Party. However, by then, the regional animosity had already torn the nation apart along geographical lines, even if both sides had similar political aspirations.

When the Democratic Convention met in April 1860 in Charleston, South Carolina, the northern Democrats selected Stephen A. Douglas of Illinois. The angered southern delegates left the convention and later named their candidate, John C. Breckinridge of Kentucky. Lincoln's victory was almost inevitable with two Democratic tickets in the running, dividing the party along the northern and southern lines. The sudden fear of the possibility of a Republican president at the head of the nation and a party deeply rooted in the free-soil doctrine of preventing the spread of slavery brought about massive condemnation from southern leaders. In a speech delivered before the Georgia House of Representatives days after the election of Abraham Lincoln, Alexander Stephens, the future vice-president of the Confederacy, stated, "Mr. Lincoln's policy and principles are against the Constitution, and…if he carries them out, it will be destructive of our rights."[3] South Carolina's Declaration of the Causes of Secession was equally blunt in stating that the electoral victory of the Republican Party had placed in power a party bent on subverting the South's right to own enslaved people. The document evoked Lincoln's own words that the "government cannot endure permanently half slave, half free." Lincoln attempted damage control after more states began to secede from the Union. He needed to solidify his platform to have the proper backing to wage war if war was necessary to bring the southern states back into the Union.

Regardless of its geographical location, New Jersey was decisively more pro-southern than any of its northern neighbors. Together with California, it was the only free-soil state to fully enforce the Fugitive Slave Law, which saw countless free Black Americans enslaved and brought back to the South as fugitives. Throughout the 1850s and well into the war years, the state's opposition was very blunt in speaking against the Republican Party, Lincoln, and the abolitionists. One of the main reasons for the Garden State's southern tendencies stemmed from its economic reliance on the South. Most of Trenton's merchants traded exclusively below the Mason-Dixon line, and Newark sent more than two-thirds of its shoes, clothing, leather goods, and carriages to the southern markets.[4] Some of these feelings stemmed from social factors, such as the countless summer visitors to the Jersey shore or half of Princeton University's students all coming from the South.

While the state was generally more Democratic, this did not mean that it lacked the nationally growing enthusiasm of the new Republican Party. In fact, the state was Republican enough to make William Dayton, a Freehold attorney, the Republican candidate for vice president in the 1856 election. Still, the Democrat, James Buchanan, would win that election with New Jersey's support. Lincoln's nomination for the presidency in the summer of 1860 awoke the bitter divisions within the state. Newspaper editors joined the fight. Papers such as the *Newark Journal*, the *Trenton Daily True American*, the *Mount Holly Herald*, and the *Sussex County New Jersey Herald* assailed Lincoln and all Republican candidates. At the same time, the *Newark Mercury*, *New Brunswick Fredonian*, and the *Tom's River Ocean Emblem* typified the staunchly pro-Republican papers.[5] The charged atmosphere led one *Mercury* editorial calling the Democrats "a band of mercenary and unprincipled men engaged in southern trade," adding that voting against Lincoln amounted to fulfilling "the wishes of their southern masters."[6]

The split Democratic ticket drew a total of 62,800 votes in New Jersey, to Lincoln's 58,000. The split, however, did garner Lincoln four of the available seven electoral votes.[7] Looking at the state's voting trends, Lincoln mainly carried the southern counties farther away from the heavily Democratic New York. Apart from the outlier Morris County in the north, the Republicans led the ballot count in Mercer, Passaic, Ocean, Burlington, Salem, Gloucester, Atlantic, Cumberland and Cape May. Still, the Garden State was not entirely out of touch with the rest of the nation, in which the new president-elect won only 40 percent of the popular vote.

A photograph of President Abraham Lincoln sitting for a portrait in Washington, D.C. *Library of Congress.*

Nonetheless, the Republicans did manage to get the majority of the electoral votes and push their man through and into the White House. When South Carolina announced its secession in late December 1860, the *Newark Journal's* editor thanked the seceding state for saving the nation from "a worse calamity than disunion—abolition!" The newspaper's front page declared, "Southern Cause Our Cause."[8] Former New Jersey governor Rodman Price urged the state to turn against Lincoln and "go with the South from every wise, prudential and patriotic reason."

The scenes in New Jersey became the most glaring repudiation of Lincoln's national victory. This was also why the president-elect purposely included the Garden State as one of the stops on his way from Springfield to Washington. With war on the horizon, Lincoln would need the manpower and industry of this densely populated northern state if he was to succeed in avoiding further renunciation of his policies once he was president of the United States. Lincoln would spend but seven hours in what the press at the time called "the northernmost of the border states." In that short time, he managed to win the goodwill of New Jersey's lawmakers and people, something that was far from a forgone conclusion when he stepped off the ferryboat *John P. Jackson* in Jersey City on February 21, 1861.

As the ferryboat docked, Lincoln was ushered into the Jersey City train depot, where all the train carts had been removed from the platforms to make way for the approximately twenty-five thousand spectators who had gathered. As he stepped onto a flag-decorated platform, a wild roar of cheers went up from the crowd, lasting for more than five full minutes. Waiting for the people's euphoria to subside, the president-elect took the time to exchange some kind words with Mayor Van Vorst and the New Jersey attorney of state William L. Dayton. After a speech was given by

Dayton, in which he welcomed Lincoln to the Garden State and said he regretted that he could only spend such a short time within its borders, the future president spoke briefly, thanking the spectators. A dissatisfied crowd cheered loudly as he stepped off the platform, "Lincoln, Lincoln!" Men and women rushed past the police officers to try to shake Lincoln's hand. With the situation getting out of hand, Lincoln returned to the platform to get all the people's attention once again. After some jokes pertaining to his seemingly new popularity with the local ladies, the tall statesman's admirers seemed to calm down. At one point, a young boy, barely four feet tall, managed to climb the platform and shake hands with Lincoln, only to be then laughed at by the crowd for being promptly thrown off the stage by a nearby officer of the law.

Lincoln was led into a special train car decorated with American and New Jersey flags. His family, including his wife and children, were already waiting for him, with the youngest boy, Tad, excited for the train ride in the car that was specially made and tailored for the presidential visit. The last thing the boy heard as the train moved out of the depot was the thirty-four-cannon salute honoring his father. The elder Lincoln made his way to the rear car, where he stepped out and waved goodbye to the cheering masses, who never seemed to disappear through the entire ride toward Newark. Men and women were perched on rooftops and treetops to get even a glimpse of the president-elect. A reporter who was given the honor of traveling with Lincoln on his trip between New York and Philadelphia via New Jersey wrote about speaking to the statesman about the surprising nature of the crowd that had so often vilified him in public and in the press. When Tad joined the conversation, he alluded to the fact that his father was surely beloved here. The elder Lincoln responded, "Uneasy sleeps the head that wears the crown." He patted his son on the head and became silent for the remainder of the ride.[9]

It was 10:30 a.m., nearly one hour after departing Jersey City when the whistle announced the train was pulling into the Newark depot. As Lincoln disembarked his car, he stepped into an open carriage and began his procession through the masses, surrounded by security guards. Newspapers reported the streets of Newark were nearly impassible, as Hackensack, Paterson, Elizabeth and hundreds of other smaller towns had sent their allocated quota of spectators. Lincoln himself remarked that the reception was unmatched by any other stop since his departure from Springfield. Women threw flowers and kisses toward the moving carriage, and thousands closed ranks behind it as it moved forward.

Yet, this was still the same New Jersey that refused the man all its electoral votes. While Lincoln waved at the masses, the lone reporter who was granted the honor of sitting in the carriage with the president-elect scribbled notes in his notepad. It was he who noticed out of the corner of his eye an "incident, significant of the popular feeling [in the state]." Suspended from a beam in the center of Newark and near the procession route hung an effigy of a man with a long black beard bearing a whip in his nerveless hand. Beneath the figure swung a board with "The Doom of Traitors" written on it in big letters.[10] Specifically taking note of Lincoln's reaction, the reporter noticed that the statesman "took but a passing notice of this device." The procession ended with a short speech, after which Lincoln once again boarded the train on his route to the state capital, Trenton.

Before arriving at its destination, the train stopped only once at Princeton University. Students came out in great numbers to surround the train tracks with cheers and salutes. An overwhelmed Lincoln ordered the train to slow down as he made his way to the back platform and waved toward the exuberant youths before continuing on toward Trenton. As the president-elect was the guest of the state, both branches of the legislature unanimously resolved to take part in his welcome. There was no doubting the fact that the atmosphere in the Democratic-controlled assembly was unfriendly toward Lincoln on the eve of his visit, with the men having spent the better part of the previous twenty-four hours making resolutions to support the South. The crowd of nearly twenty-five thousand that surrounded the train depot erupted in a cheer at noon when the whistle of the Lincoln locomotive was finally heard. German artillerists brought over from Paterson fired a national salute of thirty-four guns for just the occasion. Someone among the masses shouted, "Three cheers for Abe!" This continued to be repeated for many minutes. Lincoln was ushered into his carriage by the mayor of Trenton and a member of the city council. As the carriage left toward the statehouse, all the men in the welcoming party respectfully lifted their hats.

The procession to the state's capitol, where Lincoln was to meet the members of the legislature and other state officers, was taken up without Mrs. Lincoln and the boys. They were taken in a separate carriage to a home of a local dignitary to have an early dinner. The procession was a sight to behold. First came the mounted company of thirty volunteers carrying a massive American flag, then two companies of militia, and finally over one hundred band members bellowing out music to the pleased president-elect riding directly behind them. When the carriage finally reached the capitol building, Lincoln took a moment to shake hands with nearby citizens. Mothers held their babies over their heads all around him, fearing their children would miss an opportunity to see the future president of the Unites States. A few shouts were heard from the back of the line that needed to be quelled by the police officers. However, the overall scene seemed to be what at least one reporter called "a universal sentiment of respect and approbation for the new chief."[11]

Lincoln entered the small Senate chamber. Most onlookers, privileged to be invited, were confined to the lower-level lobby as the members sat on the perched-up floor. After listening to the senate president's greeting, the visibly tired Lincoln spoke about the importance of New Jersey in the Revolutionary War for Independence and the need for the state to then stand in defense of the very nation it once helped establish. Then came the dreaded visit to the Democratic-majority assembly chamber, where Lincoln was clearly less popular. In fact, the assemblymen were making jests and passing childish resolutions regarding the future commander in chief, even as he spoke to the senate, a few steps away from them. The chamber's minutes included resolutions: "That when this house shall have seen Abraham Lincoln, they will have seen the ugliest man in America," and "That we trust this legislature may always have a democratic member that shall exceed the president-elect by two and a half inches in height."[12] The laughing quickly seized as Lincoln quietly, as if unobtrusively, entered the chamber. What followed could make a perfect movie scene.

After thanking the senate for the warm reception that had greeted him in New Jersey and some brief remarks about the state's history, Lincoln's voice trailed away for a moment, and his eyes abandoned the prepared notes he held in his hands. "I appropriate myself very little of the demonstrations of respect with which I have been greeted. I think little should be given to any man, but that it should be a manifestation of adherence to the Union and the Constitution." A murmur of approval came from the back as others shook their heads in the affirmative. "I understand myself," he continued, "to be received here by the representatives of the people of New Jersey, a majority of whom differ in opinion from those with whom I have acted." He made it clear that he was there because of these people and not despite it them. Continuing to speak about the state's devotion to the Union, the Constitution and democracy, Lincoln was very clear with his assertion that perhaps no other state in the Union respected these sacred principles any more than New Jersey.

To his surprise, as well as perhaps to the surprise of the members of the senate themselves, the crowd began to turn. As Lincoln spoke of his desire to preserve the Union being his main objective—and not the abolition of slavery, as he was commonly accused of championing—the voices of approval grew in volume. He declared that he held "no malice toward any section" and that "the man [did] not live who [was] more devoted to peace than [he was]," and "none would do more to preserve it." And then came the unexpected. After pausing to say, "But it may be necessary to put the foot down firmly!" As noted by a reporter for the *New York Tribune*, the legislature broke into "cheers so loud and long that for some moments, it was impossible to hear Mr. L's voice."[13] Seeing that he had the senators behind him, Lincoln took off his reading glasses and placed them on the podium. Speaking softly, he stated, "And if I do my duty and do it right, you will sustain me, will you not?" The entire room seemed to erupt with a resounding "Yes! Yes! Yes! We will!" Lincoln looked up, satisfied—no, confident—that he had won New Jersey.

THE FUTURE COMMANDER IN chief left the legislative halls and resumed his journey across the Delaware River and into Pennsylvania within minutes of concluding his speech. Lincoln visited the Garden State's capital four years later, when, on his way back to Springfield, the train bearing his corpse passed through the very same towns. By then, New Jersey had sacrificed the lives of nearly six thousand men, keeping the promise it made in the assembly chamber on February 21, 1861. Yet the relationship between the Garden State and the nation's leader was far from harmonious. There is no denying the fact that Lincoln's visit to the state in 1861 did much in garnering New Jersey's support for the war that followed. Yet it would be misleading to say that the pro-South state turned around entirely toward supporting the Republican Party because of one seven-hour visit by the president-elect.

When Lincoln boarded the train from Trenton to Philadelphia, the people of New Jersey were ready to preserve the Union at all costs and follow their commander in chief. Yet that did not mean they suddenly liked him and the party he represented. When New Jersey went to war in 1861, it did so on the premise of preserving the Union, as stated in Lincoln's address to the legislature. When the federal government switched gears to focus on abolishing slavery as a means of downing the economic and social fabric of the Confederacy, the opposition toward Lincoln and the war itself was quick to resume its fervor.

As cannonballs shelled Fort Sumter in South Carolina on April 12, 1861, many New Jerseyans awoke to their neighbors stirred up into a patriotic frenzy. Men, women and children paraded in the streets as American flags hung out of open windows. Even the newspaper editors who had recently vilified Lincoln and the Republicans' stance had opened up to the idea of supporting the national cause. Over ten thousand men answered the president's April 17 call to the state to raise 3,120 volunteers.[14] The dichotomy was most striking at Princeton University. Nearly half of the student body said goodbye to their classmates and friends as they boarded trains headed South to take them to Confederate enlistment stations.

New Jersey became the model state in Lincoln's crusade to preserve the Union. While it had not a single militia member that it could speak of on April 17, within three weeks, it had fulfilled all federal obligations before any of its northern neighbors. By October, following the First Battle of Bull Run, where it became apparent that this war would last past Christmas (the miscalculated end date of seemingly all wars), the Garden State had eight regiments camped in the capital, ready for action.

By late 1861, with the then-apparent stalemate in the conflict, New Jersey's anti-Lincoln newspaper editors renewed their antiwar attacks. And by the year's end, Bergen County became the center of the state's Copperheads, or antiwar Democrats. As the casualty lists and subsequent calls for more troops from the Garden State grew, so did the strength of the opposition forces. Twenty-seven state regiments were in the field by the fall of 1862, and more than thirty thousand New Jerseyans were in Union uniforms by the winter of 1863. With more young New Jerseyans losing their lives each day, the state's Copperheads got a further boost of support after Lincoln's Emancipation Proclamation of January 1863. Resolutions to stop the war were quick to follow in the state's capitol in March 1863. The opposition was stifled in the state's congress by prowar Democrats and Lincoln Republicans, yet the seeds of dissent were evident. When the Confederate armies made it to Gettysburg, Pennsylvania, in the summer of 1863, many New Jerseyans feared that an attack on their state was possible because of its proximity. Yet, when the state governor called for militia volunteers to speed to Gettysburg to assist their state neighbors, none did, even though thousands of recently released soldiers were available.[15] A similar situation occurred in Camden and Somerset Counties, where volunteer companies disbanded when ordered to the front.

Even a victory in Gettysburg did not quell the dissent that followed the federal government's enforcement of conscription. The draft became the

A James Earle Fraser bronze statue of a young Abraham Lincoln, titled *The Candidate*, located in Jersey City, New Jersey. *Library of Congress.*

main issue of the 1864 presidential election, and Lincoln once again found himself in the hot seat in New Jersey. His first visit to the state in 1861 then seemed like it had occurred ages ago at a different time in another place. Having witnessed the carnage of war, the United States and its people would never be the same. After nearly four long years, families— not just those from New Jersey—were done sacrificing their loved ones. They wanted it all to end. Lincoln's campaign took a hit in New Jersey when he faced a man who owned property in the state, Major General George B. McClellan. He was seen as the champion of the weary troops and veterans. Having been fired by Lincoln because of his delay in pressing the issue against the Confederates following the Union victory at Antietam, "Little Mac," as his soldiers affectionately called him, accepted the Democratic nomination offered to him without delay. And although he opposed the Democratic Party's stance that the war had been a failure, McClellan nonetheless found himself representing the platform on the national presidential ticket.

It was 1864, and once again, New Jersey had rebutted Abraham Lincoln. There was no division of electoral votes this time; none would go to Lincoln. Little Mac won the state's seven electoral votes and beat the president by seven thousand votes, but his only other wins came from Kentucky and Delaware. The war would continue under Lincoln's tillage for another year. On April 10, 1865, news had finally reached New Jersey of General Robert E. Lee's surrender on April 2 to Union general Ulysses S. Grant. Thousands left their homes and packed the local churches, thankful for the fact that their family members would be coming home. The national nightmare was over, albeit for a brief moment, as the telegram ticked out the awful news of Lincoln's assassination. It would not be a celebratory Easter after all.

On April 24, 1865, Lincoln returned to New Jersey once again. This time, it was in a coffin as his funeral train passed through the state. His death added to the long tally of 218 officers and 6,082 enlisted men from New Jersey who died in the bloodiest war the nation had ever seen. Newspapers would report New Jersey's silent cries and mournful faces that came out to see the train on that rainy day. New Jersey historian John T. Cunningham would later write of the president's final visit: "Lincoln, in death, had conquered New Jersey as he had not done in life."[16] In the end, the anti-Republican feelings and tendencies that were briefly suspended by the allure of Abraham Lincoln's visits to the state—first in life in February 1861 and then in death in April 1865—quickly returned. As the Civil War made way for Reconstruction, the state legislature refused to ratify the Thirteenth Amendment and end slavery. This time, there was no Lincoln to inspire them to change their minds, as he had once managed to do for just a brief moment in February 1861.

THE JERSEY SHORE OF GRANT, HARRISON AND OTHERS

Long before President Donald Trump visited the Jersey shore for his working vacation in 2017 at the Bedminster Trump National Golf Club, the Jersey shore, with its miles of sunny beaches and glamorous resorts, was already the go-to summer destination for American presidents. It began with Cape May, an early go-to for the rich and famous—commanders in chief included—and eventually spread up the shoreline into Long Branch, which was made popular by none other than Ulysses S. Grant. It did not take long for Cape May to hold the title of the most fashionable resort on the Jersey shore. As the wealthy continued to flock there as early as the turn of the nineteenth century, the resort town peaked shortly before the Civil War. In 1850 alone, seventeen thousand visitors graced its hotels and resorts. By the late 1800s, at least five United States presidents had spent time in the resort town, most choosing the grandeur of Congress Hall. The tradition began with Franklin Pierce in the 1840s, and he was followed by James Buchanan, Ulysses S. Grant, Chester Arthur and Benjamin Harrison. Grant and Harrison later decided to turn the Jersey shore into a more permanent "summer White House."

It is no wonder that Cape May attracted the American commander in chief in the 1840s. Families of well-to-do businessmen took time off from their stressful New York, Philadelphia and Baltimore jobs and set out to spend their summers in the enormous Victorian hotels that were built there for entertaining. The larger homes competed to offer the best attractions, the biggest of which was dancing to live music in grand ballrooms and eating in large dining halls. Wide hotel porches furnished with rockers and sitting areas where one could have a drink or play cards allowed for social gatherings. The larger hotels, such as the Mount Vernon Hotel or Congress Hall, boasted that their pianos were special instruments, "most of which came from Vienna and had that peculiar tone which they caught from the damp sea air, which rusted the wire and softened the dampers and made the music sound like the blowing of the northeast wind through a girl's wet hair."[17] Apart from sea bathing and frequenting gambling halls, vacationers at Cape May spent a significant amount of time people-watching and talking about who's who. The streets were full of beautiful purebred horses and imported carriages with famous teams of coachmen driving around the wealthy vacationers on their afternoon excursions from their private mansions. On their daily drives, ladies dressed in wide skirts shielded their light complexions with small parasols, "creations of silk and lace with handles adjustable to any angle." The drives were more of a formal affair and involved an awful lot of courtly bows and hat-tipping.

It was this environment that welcomed the first president down to Cape May, beginning the tradition for many others. Franklin Pierce, the fourteenth president of the United States (serving his term between 1853 and 1857), visited the famous Congress Hall Hotel for the Fourth of July weekend in 1855, much to the dismay of his political opponents. After a public reception that saw visitors come from far and away to see the commander in chief speak, Pierce and his wife settled into their quick weekend getaway. But there was nothing happy about the excursion. Pierce's life reflected the doomed national situation of the time. With relations between the North and South pushed to the brink by the Compromise of 1850, the Fugitive Slave Act, and the publication of *Uncle Tom's Cabin*, which both sides viewed as either attacking or defending slavery, it was a precarious time for the president to take a vacation. These tensions were exacerbated by the situation in Kansas between proslavery and antislavery factions, which had just turned violent the month of this trip. The *New York Times* made the nation's frustration known in an editorial, which complained that with the country at a critical moment, it had "lost its president." Smirkingly, the writer wrote, "President Pierce is at Cape May, [but] for practical reasons, he might as well be at Cape Horn [in Africa].[18]

The Pierces' time at the White House began with a tragedy that would come to define the next four years of their lives in the national spotlight. It would ultimately lead to the president's heavy drinking and would see him die from liver cirrhosis by the end of the following decade. When nominated

A porch of Cape May's Congress Hall, which many American presidents frequented during the nineteenth century. *Library of Congress.*

by the Democratic Party in 1852 for the presidential election, which he would come to win by a majority vote, Franklin's wife fainted at the news. Even his only surviving child, eleven-year-old Benny (his two other children died in childbirth), wrote to his mother that he had hoped his father would not win. So, the one-term presidency of a northerner who was supportive of a southern cause but who was unable to please either seemed to be cursed from the start. Shortly after Pierce won the election, the family took a trip from Andover, New Hampshire. The train they were traveling on was derailed, resulting in a crash that took Benny's life. The shocked president-elect rushed to his son's limp body that a piece of wood had just struck, only to find the boy's head crushed beyond recognition. The parents never got over the death of their third and only living child. Historian James Morgan wrote, "Presidential honors were never less welcome than in that of the Pierces."

Because of the grief and deep depression of his wife, Pierce decided on a stay at the Jersey shore in 1855. Following the tragic accident, Jane Pierce saw the death of her son as a divine interference connected to her husband's summons to the nation's highest office. She even blocked a lawsuit against the train company so as not to disturb the supposed act of God. When Pierce took the oath of office a couple of months later, he refused to swear on the Bible, blaming Benny's death on God's judgment of him taking the post. Jane would spend the first half of Franklin's presidency mourning, refusing all political and social responsibilities. Yet her constant depression and a bout with tuberculosis left the first lady wanting a break from the business of the capital. And the president, himself battling with post-traumatic stress disorder and depression, saw Cape May as the perfect place for a Fourth of July getaway.

Due to Pierces' private nature, not much is known about how they spent their time at the Jersey shore, apart from the fact that it did stir the press on both sides. As the New York papers continued to begrudge the president's choice to take time off during the hostilities in Kansas, the *Washington Evening Star*'s editor came to his defense: "Has it come to this, that a president of the United States cannot visit the seaside with a member of his family, to whom the fresh and invigorating ocean air is essential to the recovery of health, without incurring the malignant mendacity of partisan newspapers?"[19]

Although he was the first, Pierce was undoubtedly not the last president to choose the Jersey shore as a summer destination. And even though their stays were shorter and thus not necessarily more significant than Pierce's, the men did leave enough of a mark to warrant mentioning. James Buchanan, who followed Franklin into the White House, chose the same vacation spot as his predecessor, arriving in Cape May for a few days in 1858. It was noted that the president detested Washington, D.C.'s stuffy air and often complained of the White House's "bad vapors." In fact, he refused to spend summer nights in the presidential mansion, choosing instead to sleep at the nearby soldiers' home cottage. Buchanan would return to the seaside resort town once more years after the Civil War. However, by then, his reputation as one of history's worst presidents for letting the South secede after Lincoln's 1860 election had tarnished his image enough to make his visit very low-key.

Another president who made stops at Cape May and the famed Congress Hall was none other than President Grant. Although he would later choose Long Branch as his more permanent summer place, it was Cape May where the most famous man in the nation at the time, hailed as the victor of the Civil War, made his first visit to the Jersey shore. The 1869 stop would mark the first of four trips that Grant would eventually make to the seaside town. The proprietor of Congress Hall, who was in charge of the ceremonies, planned for a handful of town council members to greet the president at the railroad station where he was scheduled to deliver an address. Yet when they showed up looking less glamorous and worse dressed than he anticipated, the master of ceremonies dismissed them and substituted the council with nine of the best-looking guests he could find in his hotel. In a humorous turn of events, one of the random men who played the role of the mayor delivered the welcome address and presided over the evening's entire banquet—all without Grant's knowledge.[20] Apparently, the hotel proprietor had enough influence with the media to keep the whole incident out of the local papers.

Grant's visit was reminiscent of Lincoln's nearly a decade before. The crowds numbering in thousands, starved to get a glimpse of their leader, filled the relatively small seaside town to see the man as he reviewed military drills conducted by Camp Union troops on the Congress Hall lawn. Newspapers, thirsty for any news of the visit, printed such minuscule details of the event as Mrs. Grant ordering two bathing outfits, "one in red flannel trimmed in blue, the other blue trimmed in red."[21] Although the visit started most splendidly, with booming cannons and the regatta filled with more men and women than the town had ever witnessed, the staff at Congress Hall would later complain of Grant's less than exemplary behavior, especially when it came to their food. The president proved to be a picky eater, insisting that his meat be returned to the kitchen and cooked again, this time to a crunch, something he would do regardless of the meat type—that is, except chicken, which he refused to eat altogether.[22] The distaste and boredom painted on Mrs. Grant's face made it that much less shocking when the Grants chose the up-and-coming Long Branch, Cape May's biggest competitor for the title of the most exclusive resort as their more permanent settlement during the subsequent summers.

By the time Chester A. Arthur visited Cape May in 1883, there was no denying the significance of the Jersey shore as the go-to presidential summer stop. The president and his daughter arrived on a government steamer on July 24 to a crowd estimated by the *New York Times* to have been ten thousand strong.[23] Making his way through the town in a fashionable carriage that fit the occasion and the glamour of Cape May, Arthur was stopped in front of Congress Hall by the huge masses of people who clamored to shake the president's hand, which, reportedly, he gladly obliged. Following the evening banquet and ball given in his honor, the commander in chief was rowed to his steamer the *Dispatch* amid a dramatically "great display of fireworks," accompanied by loud music and cheer.[24]

Like Grant, Benjamin Harrison's brief stay at the Jersey shore would turn into more extended stays throughout the summer months of his presidency. However, instead of Long Branch, which was the general's choice, Harrison was impressed enough by his first visit to Cape May to make it the location of his permanent summer White House years later. The president's first visit to the resort town was in 1889, when he stopped by his postmaster general and Philadelphia department state mogul, John Wannamaker's home. He was accompanied on his trip by some famous people, including Secretary of State James G. Blaine and General William T. Sherman.[25] Entertained for nearly a week by the exceedingly wealthy John Wannamaker, Harrison and his first lady, Caroline, spent each night at various balls and banquets and thoroughly enjoyed the fresh seafood offered at each turn. The first lady was also very impressed with Cape May's ocean views and gardens as an artist and painter. It was only a matter of time before she and her husband would turn the resort town into their summer residence.

Apart from Grant, two presidents who would grace the Jersey beaches with their presence (like the Civil War general, farther north from Cape May near Long Branch), were Rutherford B. Hayes and Woodrow Wilson. Long Branch, which, by the 1860s, had become a fashionable resort town in its own right, was made into a permanent summer presidential residence by Ulysses S. Grant in the 1870s and would again be thrust into the spotlight by President James Garfield, who died there in 1881. Yet its story did not end there. Grant's successor, President Hayes, and his wife often came up to the resort town and stayed in the elegant Elberton Hotel. Yet the stoic couple seldom solicited much excitement from the locals, and as stated by New Jersey historian Harold F. Wilson, "Considerably less dazzling than Grant, the sole contribution of President and Mrs. Hayes to the social scene was their presence."[26] In the early twentieth century, President Woodrow Wilson would also spend many days "working from home" at his summer cottage, the Shadow Lawn, near Long Branch. *Cottage* is perhaps a little misleading, as the colonial home had over fifty rooms and was surrounded by beautifully elaborate porches from which the president would give press briefings and even accept his nominations for the presidency, both in 1912 and 1916. He spent both elections nights sleeping at his shore home, waiting for the winning results.

THE MOST PROMINENT PRESIDENTIAL visits, or rather extended vacations, to the Jersey shore that made the presidents' time in New Jersey seem significant came from the two times the sandy beaches of the Garden States were turned into a summer White House. First, it would be Grant in Long Branch, and then Harrison would follow in Cape May. For a few brief summer months throughout the two men's presidencies, the nation's eyes would be turned toward New Jersey.

Long Branch began to take business away from Cape May in the mid-nineteenth century, as it became known for being more playful. While Cape May was still all about being prim and proper, Long Branch was more of a high-end entertainment center of the Jersey shore. By 1860, nearly five thousand hotels and boardinghouses accommodated card playing, billiards, bowling and fast horse carriage racing down the beach. Apart from stays by

A photograph of President Grant, his wife, Julia, and son Jesse at his Long Branch cottage on the shores of New Jersey. *Library of Congress.*

famous actors, including Edwin Booth and Maggie Mitchell, other notable guests included Mexican war hero General Winfield Scott and Mrs. Lincoln, who vacationed in Long Branch in August 1861. Some would comment on the poor timing of the vacation, because when the first lady was going to a concert or watching a cricket match or water exhibition, the Union and Confederate forces were killing each other at the Civil War's First Battle of Bull Run.[27]

The real draw to the area famously known for its entertainment and horseracing, which would result in property values soaring from $500 to $5,000 an acre, came courtesy of President Ulysses S. Grant, who turned the town into his personal summer White House. Attracted to the area by its reputation for gaming, overall gayness and horse racing, of which he was a big fan, Grant first brought his wife and children to Long Branch in the summer of 1869. Having previously stayed at Cape May, farther south, the Grants took more of a liking to the slightly less formal atmosphere in the more northern resort town.

The first couple initially tried two of the poshest hotels, the Mansion House and the Stetson, but grew to dislike the formality associated with their stays there. As if being ridiculed for his lack of dancing skills was not enough, the president hated being subjected to dressing in broadcloth and standing on the piazza, bowing and smiling at ladies passing by.[28] Thousands flocked to Long Branch to catch a glimpse of the president. It seemed like overnight, the town became the newest New Jersey shore go-to destination for celebrities, society leaders and the wealthy. President Grant may not have been too ecstatic about all the attention, but it did not prevent him from loving Long Beach. In a letter to his friend, he plainly stated, "Never [have I] seen a place in all [my] travels which was better suited for a summer residence." Grant was miserable in Washington, D.C.'s, summer humidity, not to mention the endless number of callers who lined up on the White House stairs every morning. It was time for a summer residence, and Long Branch fit the bill.

In a move that followed what historians would later brand as the president's gullible tendency of trusting the many corrupt capitalists around him, in 1869, Grant accepted a gift of a summer cottage built for him by famous millionaires of the time George W. Childs, George Pullman and Moses Taylor. The house at 991 Ocean Avenue was built in an English villa style and was wrapped around by a porch from which the president could enjoy the ocean views. Grant would spend each summer as president at his New Jersey retreat unless he was traveling. When he was not working or entertaining

President Grant's cottage at Long Branch as it looked when it served as the official summer White House for the eighteenth president. *Library of Congress.*

from his porch, he spent time at the Pennsylvania Club and the New York Club, high-end gambling establishments. In the former, between $5 million and $10 million were waged there in a single summer season, making it the premier gambling destination.[29] The president's other famous pastime was frequenting the nearby Monmouth Park Racetrack, with a grandstand that seated thousands of people. The town was becoming sort of a Las Vegas of its time, and Grant was thoroughly enjoying his summer capital as a perfect escape from the sweltering atmosphere of Washington, D.C.

Aside from swimming at his private beachfront, Grant would often spend his mornings racing his horses Egypt and Cincinnati down the Long Branch shore or enjoying the company of the rich and famous on his porch. The president was often caught sitting with a cigar in his mouth in the shade of his porch, wearing a white plug hat and a linen duster, talking to some guest of his choice. There were visits from known American generals, such as Gordon Meade and Phil Sheridan, and the president had conversations with the wealthiest locals, such as Henry Van Brunt. The latter owned the bathing pavilion directly opposite the fashionable Mansion House.[30] That is not to say that the president was not seen around town. In fact, it was almost a foregone conclusion that one would catch a glimpse of the nation's leader coming down the street in his horse and buggy for a leisurely drive down Ocean Avenue, Long Branch's main strip.

Grant would continue to see the Jersey shore as his getaway, even after his presidency ended. When faced with a political scandal in which he unknowingly, or rather ignorantly, invested in a Wall Street company that would bankrupt him and tarnish his reputation, the general once again returned to his cottage in Long Branch. The summer of 1884 was very unlike the previous summers, as the Grants were forced to let go of all their help, prompting the former first lady to cook and clean around the house. It was in Long Branch that, after a month of staring disconsolately at the ocean, Grant, at the suggestion of Mark Twain, began writing his classic memoirs, which he completed at a heartbreaking pace before dying from throat cancer in 1885.[31]

Another president who, between 1889 and 1893, chose to turn the Jersey shore into a summer white house—albeit in the original and classic glamour of Cape May—was Benjamin Harrison. His stay would elicit some condemnation from his political adversaries, who accused Harrison's gift of a summer home from the wealthy Philadelphia department store mogul John Wanamaker as a financial bribe. After President Harrison appointed Wanamaker his postmaster general, the accusations only grew in volume.

The Grant Cottage from
995 Ocean Avenue,
Long Branch as it looked
shortly before it was
demolished in the 1930s.
Library of Congress.

After a brief summer stint in Cape May in 1889, Mrs. Harrison was smitten
with the resort town, prompting her to press the president to accept the gift
of a summer cottage from the postmaster general and his wealthy associates.
What made matters worse was the fact that to the locals and, soon, the
international press, Wanamaker and his wealthy backers were unofficially
known as the "syndicate."

Their intentions were not the purest. The "syndicate" sped up the
construction of the twenty-three-room mansion for the president, mainly to
use him as an attraction for larger crowds and more considerable publicity
for the resort town. Having his reservations about public perception,
Harrison initially refused the gift, only to have the wealthy benefactors
publicly gift it to his wife in June 1890. Foreseeing backlash from the press,
the president sent Wanamaker a check for $10,000 with a note thanking him
for constructing a beautiful summer home. Yet, as foreseen, the second the
Harrisons moved in, the press had a field day. Washington papers labeled the
whole exchange a scandal, with headlines proclaiming that the "syndicate"
had bought presidential favor for railroad and housing developers.[32]

Regardless of the pushback, the Harrisons settled into their new summer
home right away. In retrospect, this was more of a Mrs. Harrison affair than
an act of the president. And although he spent the next two summers at the
Cape May home, it was First Lady Caroline Harrison who became more
of an attraction for the oceanside town. She would personally send in and
receive food orders as if she was just another resident. Also intrigued by the
picturesque Cape May, Mrs. Harrison would often be seen taking carriage
rides around the neighboring countryside, sometimes with her husband. Dan

and Judy Kelly, who owned a small cottage near the old brick Presbyterian church in Cold Spring, where the Harrisons attended mass every Sunday, were quite surprised when the president knocked on their door and asked for a glass of water. Lady Caroline was taken aback by Kelly's property and wished to stop the carriage to take in the beautiful scenery. Upon leaving, the president thanked Mrs. Kelly and pressed a five-dollar bill into her hand.[33]

Wanamaker was not incorrect in thinking that having the president of the United States living in Cape May throughout the summer—both in 1890 and 1891—would attract more attention to the already known town. This effect was only strengthened when the president, wanting to separate work from home, decided to commission the first floor of the famed Congress Hall as the official summer White House in 1891. The decision was made that this was much easier, as the White House was being rewired for electricity that summer and construction crews made working there that much more difficult. Once at Cape May full-time, Harrison's professional life was confined to the hotel's offices. Still, his private life continued to draw attention. An item appearing in the *New York Herald* on July 12, 1891, indicated the interest that was taken in every aspect of the president's life: "It is in his bathing suit, bare-legged, armed and headed, that Mr. Harrison shows his improvements in physique to the best advantage."[34] When not working, the president was often seen taking long walks on the beach, and each weekend, the family hosted a party that would often culminate with a fireworks display.

The Harrisons did not return to their oceanside home after the summer of 1891. Following the death of Caroline from tuberculosis in 1892, the cottage would remain empty. Benjamin Harrison would sell the house back to Wanamaker in 1896 for the same $10,000 he initially paid for it. The year 1891 also marked a bittersweet moment for Cape May's Congress Hall, as this was the last time an active president walked its halls.

THERE IS PERHAPS NO denying that President Donald Trump set out to make his Trump National Golf Club in Bedminster the new summer White House. And although much of the media pointed to the blatant use of his position to bring attention to his own private business, history shows that this was by no means the only time a president's Jersey shore vacation brought about indignation from the press. Ironically, in 2018, President Trump, like one of his predecessors who vacationed on the same shores, used White House renovations as the reason for his extended stay at the shore. In his defense, the daily descriptions of his stay pointed to the man's motto that there is no vacation in business, with a stream of business calls and visits throughout the day. His afternoons were spent entertaining a slew of famous visitors, not unlike what was once done by President Grant at his Long Brach summer home. And like Chester A. Arthur, who found a moment for dancing entertainment during his brief stay at the shore, President Trump managed to squeeze in a round or two of golf. And not unlike President Franklin Pierce, Trump surely felt the air of condemnation about his time down at the Jersey shore from the press and the media. Some things most certainly do not change.

GARFIELD'S TWELVE DAYS IN JERSEY

The Garden State can claim at least one president who was born within its borders and at least two others who called the state home for a prolonged time. Yet none of those stories come close to the spectacle that became the last twelve days that President James Garfield spent in Elberon, New Jersey, right up to his death on September 19, 1881. The entire story surrounding the reason for his stay at the Jersey shore reads like a dramedy. And although there indeed should be nothing comical about one's death, especially the death of a national leader, there are many small caveats and blunders that solicit a bit of a chuckle about the sheer ignorance of the times when researching the assassination of President Garfield. This attack led to eight weeks of pain and medical mismanagement that would eventually see him die from his wound, which was easily treatable by twentieth-century standards. It was because of the president's quickly—or rather slowly—deteriorating health that his doctors suggested he relocate to the Garden State's many beaches to help lower his fevers perpetuated by Washington, D.C.'s unbearable summer heat. And thus began the story of an American president who came to New Jersey to die—all pretenses aside.

James Garfield could have been a great American President. Initially born into poverty in a log cabin in Ohio, young James became a well-educated and successful attorney before rising to the rank of major general during the Civil War. His military accolades translated to his public life, as he was elected to nine terms as a congressman from Ohio. In November 1880, General Garfield became the only president up to that point—and for the next forty years—to step directly from the Capitol to the White House. Historian James Morgan would highlight the man's executive inexperience and lack of support toward the longstanding spoils system of granting the winning party supporters office jobs. "He groaned under the rude jostling of a sordid mob of office seekers." Morgan would also point out the president's famous quote: "My God! What is there in this place that a man should ever want to get into it?"[35]

One deranged Republican, Charles Guiteau, traveled to the White House in the spring of 1881 to ask for a job on the basis of his party loyalty, only to be rejected. It was becoming evident within the first month of taking office in March 1881 that President Garfield, a man often blamed for being too honest, did not believe in the spoils system. Guiteau found that out the hard way. Yet the young man would not be dissuaded, even after being repeatedly turned away. Believing that he would perhaps have a better chance of getting a job from Vice President Chester A. Arthur, the disgruntled young man decided to speed up the transition process and his chances by shooting the president three months into his term. James Garfield would die weeks later from his wounds but not before spending his last few days on this earth breathing in the Jersey shore air.

It was the beginning of the summer of 1881 when Lucretia Garfield contracted malaria and possibly spinal meningitis, which saw her bedridden with a high temperature and briefly fighting for her life. When the fever finally broke in early June, the White House doctor recommended that she recover at a place with plenty of salty air to assist with her breathing. Going along with what by then appeared to be a presidential precedent, the Garfields headed for Long Branch on June 18. While the president would only stay briefly to see his wife made comfortable in a hotel in the Elberon section of Long Branch, Mrs. Garfield would remain at the hotel until July 2, the day she received the terrible news of her husband's injury. James Garfield returned on the train back to Washington only to be forced to travel again a few short weeks later when he was invited to deliver a speech at Williams College. Enraged by his latest denial of the post of U.S. ambassador to France, Charles Guiteau spent weeks shadowing the president's every move around town and in the newspapers. That day, he would not miss the president, figuratively or literally.

President Garfield and his secretary of state, James G. Blaine, arrived at the Baltimore and Potomac Train Depot on the morning of July 2, 1881, without much fanfare. According to witness accounts and the newspaper reports of the time, the president was barely out of his carriage and passing through the ladies' room to the train cars—back when women had their own waiting room prior to boarding—when the crazed young man emerged from the corner and fired his first shot at Garfield's back. As the surprised president made no move to shield himself, Guiteau fired his second shot. Garfield dropped to the floor as the waiting room attendee, one Mrs. White, rushed to him and raised his head. The shaken-up Blaine continuously asked Garfield if he was all right. Blood was pouring onto the dirty floor from under the seemingly lifeless commander in chief.

Meanwhile, Guiteau's escape out of the depot was very short-lived, as a ticket agent jumped out of his ticket window and tackled him to the ground. Not resisting an arrest and proclaiming that he had shot the president for the good of the country, the mentally unstable man held on to the letter addressed to General William Sherman. In it, he admitted to what he considered to be a necessary killing and asked the general to ready the troops to storm the jail he would be taken to and save the Republican Party.

With the assassin secured, attentions turned to the president, who was promptly carried up the stairs to a separate area. A known local physician, Dr. D. Willard Bliss, was called to the scene by the secretary of war, who also happened to be present at the train depot. In the first twist of irony in the case of Garfield's assassination, this position was filled by Robert Tod Lincoln, the son of the first assassinated American president. With his pulse weak and going in and out of consciousness, Garfield seemed to be following in Lincoln's footsteps. In another twist of irony—and although the omen would not be realized for another eight weeks—the city postmaster who was present at the scene of the shooting was quoted as saying, "I have been in many battles and have seen many men mortally wounded and never one with a face that more clearly showed certain death than the president's."[36]

Having assessed that it was really just one bullet that had entered the president's back that was worrisome, Dr. Bliss poked a metal probe into the wound to locate it. After an unsuccessful probing, with the president in visible pain, Bliss ordered that the commander in chief be taken back to the White House, where he would be carried upstairs and laid out in his bedroom. Soon, his bedside was surrounded by the most prominent American physicians and surgeons of their time. Looking around at the parade of doctors looming over him, Garfield asked those around him to take off his shoes, as the tingling and pain in his feet was causing the most discomfort. This would later be attributed to the bullet being lodged near his spine. When he was finally made somewhat comfortable, the visibly ailing Garfield spoke to his secretary: "Go right now and send a telegram to Mrs. Garfield saying that I feel considerably better, and if she feels well enough, tell her to come to Washington immediately."[37]

It seems that New Jersey features prominently and quite early in the events surrounding President Garfield's death. Within minutes of the event in Washington, D.C., Lucretia Garfield heard a knock on her hotel room door in Elberon, New Jersey. She grabbed the piece of telegram paper and opened it. "The president wishes me to say to you from him that he has been seriously hurt—how seriously he cannot yet say. He is himself and hopes you will come to him soon."[38] As she attempted to question the man standing in the hallway who delivered the note about the severity of her husband's injury, Mrs. Garfield was surprised to see former president Ulysses S. Grant walking down the hallway toward her room. The truth of the matter was that while the Grants were quietly staying at their son's summer cottage down the street from the hotel, they had hardly said one word to Mrs. Garfield or the president when he arrived with her a few weeks prior. The feud between the former and current president went back to the early days of Garfield's term, a few months earlier, when he granted a cabinet position to a man opposite of the one endorsed and recommended by Grant.

None of that mattered on July 2, 1881, however, as former U.S. president, Ulysses S. Grant, having himself learned of the assassination from a former supporter in Washington, stood at Mrs. Garfield's doorstep mere moments after she received the news. He took Lucretia's hand and, while clearly shaken up himself, informed her that he had just received a message from Washington that the president's wounds did not seem to be mortal and that he knew of many soldiers who had survived such injuries that then befell Garfield.[39] His intent was not to belittle the significance of the commander in chief's precarious situation but to try to comfort the grief-stricken Mrs. Garfield. Within an hour, the first lady was on a specially commissioned train pulling a solitary Pullman car, speeding out of New Jersey and toward the White House and her husband. Little did she suspect at the time that she would be bringing him back to the Garden State in a few weeks for the final twelve days of his life.

The days and weeks that followed were excruciating for the ailing president and the nation that hung on every detailed piece of information printed in the press about his health. An observer would comment that in the

Top: A picture of the Elberon cabin, where President James Garfield spent his final days looking out on the Atlantic Ocean. *Library of Congress*.

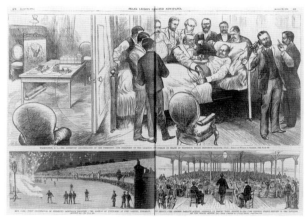

Bottom: Newspaper prints showing Alexander Graham Bell using his induction-balance device (metal detector) to locate the bullet in President Garfield's body while he lay dying in New Jersey. The other images show fireworks displays that were given in the president's honor and an evening service for his health at Asbury Park, New Jersey. *Library of Congress*.

days and weeks directly following the assassination attempt, "in every city, in every town, in every village of the United States, groups formed about the telegraph and newspaper offices and other centers of information and discussed in excited fashion the terrible news."[40] The next two months saw the doctors concerning themselves with trying to locate the second bullet to find out what organ it might have punctured (the first bullet that had grazed the president's arm was by then a nonissue). The search was conducted using various hands and unsanitary fingers, and the probes were excessive, puncturing Garfield's liver. As part of this state-of-the-art treatment, the famous inventor Alexander Graham Bell arrived at the White House with a primitive metal detector, only to mistake a metal spring in the president's mattress for the supposed bullet in his abdomen.

Convinced that the bullet had pierced Garfield's intestine, Doctor Bliss, whose name was ironically actually "Doctor," decided to switch the president to an all-liquid diet of broth, egg yolks, and whiskey.[41] As the president's fever refused to break and his weight began to drop (he would go from 200 to 130 pounds in just under six weeks), the doctors added food and opium enemas containing beef extracts and whiskey to his treatment. Yet, and perhaps unsurprisingly, Garfield's condition continued to worsen. After weeks of seeing the president in this condition and with his fever still refusing to break, Bliss concluded that the unbearably hot summer in the capital was not doing Garfield any good; the president needed to be moved to a cooler climate. A special train was commissioned to bring the American president back to the Jersey Shore.

LIKE EVERYTHING ELSE CONCERNING the president, the train fitted to take Garfield to New Jersey on September 6, 1881, was front-page news. Bliss was apprehensive about moving his patient, but the president would not hear of staying and insisted on traveling to Long Branch. When informed of the preparations for his trip, Garfield exclaimed, "I have seen men sicker than I moved without any such fuss."[42] And when looking at the excursion, the word *fuss* perhaps seems fitting. A special three-car train was brought in; there was a car that was explicitly designated for the physicians, one for the staff and one for the president. The latter contained a wooden bedframe with springs to cushion the ride, a few easy chairs for the doctors and not much else apart from a thick carpet to lessen the noise. The engine selected to pull the cars was picked for being a hard coal burner, a style that gives off almost no smoke and very little dust or ash.[43] The conductor, who would make the trip exceptionally comfortable for Garfield, was also specially selected as one of the most expert engineers employed by the Pennsylvania Railroad Company. The president would depart for his last trip to New Jersey from the same station that brought about his downfall months earlier.

The train ride itself was thoroughly planned out so as not to disturb the president. A message was sent to all conductors traveling that day between the capital and New Jersey to stop their engines as Garfield's special train was approaching. Bliss justified the orders as a means of not having the president disturbed. He also secured private people's homes along the routes in case his patient needed to stop and rest from the journey.[44] He could not foresee the thousands of people who would turn out to see the train pass through their towns. Nearly every station was filled with spectators wanting to catch a glimpse of the train that they all suspected was taking the nation's leader to his death on the New Jersey shores.

Meanwhile, in the Elberon section of Long Branch, local volunteers had constructed a nearly one-mile-long train track from the train station to the Franklyn Cottage, the twenty-odd-room seaside cottage donated by a wealthy New Yorker for Garfield's use. Laying the spur of track in the most direct route forced the engineer to run it through a woman's garden, only to have her proclaim that she did not mind. "I am willing that you should ruin my house," she told the young man, "All I have—if it would help to save him."[45] In a twist of fate, the 3,200 feet of track, while it found the quickest way from the station to the cottage, could not avoid the natural topography of the seaside mansion being situated on a hill. With the final destination in sight, the train stopped in its tracks, unable to make it the last few hundred yards. Out of nowhere, hundreds of New Jerseyans who had waited to see the arrival of their president grabbed the train cars and began to help slowly push them up the hill.

It was later reported that once he was brought into his room at the Franklyn Cottage, the president was pleased to see the countless bouquets, which helped him quickly forget the "sewage smell" of the capital.[46] He was also adamant about having the bed turned toward the window so he could look at the Atlantic Ocean and feel the breeze. Much to the president's delight, this was later amended when he was moved for hours at a time into a chair near the open window. In the days and weeks that followed, Garfield's New Jersey cottage was flooded with messages of prayers and hopes of a full recovery from all over the world. As touched as he was by the outpouring of support, he was most overcome with emotion upon finding out that a fund was being raised for his wife in the case of his death. The president was similarly grateful to his doctors, especially Dr. Bliss. Seeing that his caretaker was exhausted a few days into his stay in New Jersey, the dying president tried to comfort the physician: "Doctor, you plainly show the effect of all this care and unrest," he stated. "Your anxious watching will soon be over."[47] Yet Bliss refused to give up, going as far as to send false hope not only his patient but also to the American people. The message from Long Branch was that the president was recovering, but that could not have been further from the truth.

While the support did much to raise his spirits, the president was fading. Not many people saw Garfield during his last days at the Jersey shore, especially not the residents. His stay was not a big spectacle, with parades and ribbons. People respected his need for peace and tranquility; no one kidded themselves about what was happening at Franklyn Cottage. The doctors issued bulletins in local papers about the president's health each day. The public was flooded with unprecedented details of the executive's

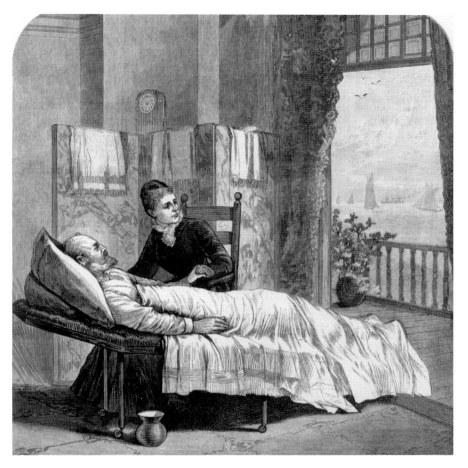

An image that appeared in the local papers when President Garfield was transported to Elberon, New Jersey. It shows the ailing leader looking out on the Jersey Shore. *Library of Congress.*

health, like his daily temperature, the amount of sleep he got, how much pus his wound discharged and even the regularity of his bowel movements. Newspapers became the only window into Garfield's last days in New Jersey, profiling not only his health but also the state of his wife and children, always by his bedside. Some responded to the articles with their own editorials and suggestions. One memorable writer suggested the president could perhaps be saved if the doctors hung him upside down to allow the bullet to fall out of him.[48] Yet it all proved futile.

On Monday, September 19, 1881, James A. Garfield woke up, content to spend his day calmly watching the sunrise, observing the waves of the ocean and the golden sand of the Jersey shore—it would be the last sunrise he ever saw. After falling asleep late in the afternoon, the president woke up in cold sweat around 10:00 p.m. He placed his hand over his chest and yelled out in terrible pain. Garfield pleaded with his secretary to make the pain disappear—all to no avail. "Can't you stop this?" croaked the president. And then there was silence. A Black servant ran to get Doctor Bliss, who was resting next door. He returned with the servant, carrying a candle, and he asked the servant to hold it over the Garfield. Bliss observed, "the pallor, the upturned eyes, the gasping respiration and the total unconsciousness" of the president.[49] The doctor looked up, "My God," he said to those in the room, "the president is dying!" After pressing his ear to his patient's chest, Bliss officially proclaimed President James A. Garfield dead at 10:35 p.m. Men passed in and out of the room for the next hour as Mrs. Garfield sat silently in the president's chair, looking at the lifeless figure that was once her husband. Outside the open window behind her, she could hear the waves crashing into the New Jersey shoreline.

"EXCITEMENT IN LONG BRANCH!" screamed the headline of the *Boston Post*, dated September 20, 1881. The news spread quickly in the seaside town, and crowds gathered almost immediately, "frantic with grief and heaping oaths loud and deep on the head of the villain Guiteau." Crowds near the cottage had to be dispersed for the arrival of Eugene Britton of Long Branch, the coroner of Monmouth County who came for the inquest. Members of the presidential cabinet began showing up at the Elberon Station late that same night, followed shortly after midnight by a train carrying the new president, Chester A. Arthur. For the next twenty-four hours, Long Brach and Elberon would grace the front pages of every major American newspaper as bulletins flew out of the seaside resort town at ferocious speeds. The crowd around the cottage began to expand all through the night, and soon, the U.S. military had to be called out to help control it. And while everyone awaited the news of what was to follow, many in attendance were relieved to find out that Mrs. Garfield had refused the requests of several cities, such as Philadelphia or Pittsburg, to have the president's body lay in state there. Instead, he would go directly from New Jersey to Washington and then to his burial place back in Ohio.

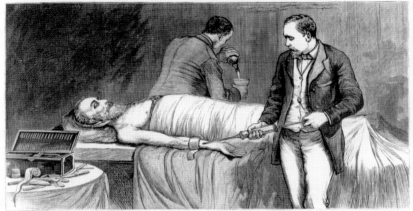

A newspaper article depicting the death of President Garfield titled "Incidents in Elberon." It shows the funeral train departing New Jersey and discusses its route. *Library of Congress.*

In the afternoon of the next day, as the military helped contain the crowds outside, and men, including doctors and a museum curator, assembled at the Franklyn Cottage for President Garfield's autopsy. It was evening before the doctors finally found out that they were wrong the whole time about the location of the bullet that killed the president. Instead of the right front side of the president's torso, the bullet had actually lodged itself on the left side of Garfield's chest. Across the street from the cottage, one could see many onlookers on the porch of the Elberon Hotel, hoping to get a glimpse of the dreadful affair. They and the world would soon find out that the president had died from a terrible case of septic poisoning. The following day, on Wednesday, September 21, the president's body was loaded onto the same specialty train that had brought him to Elberon. He was escorted to the station by the governor of New Jersey, where the grieving Mrs. Garfield and her children were met by the newly sworn-in president Chester A. Arthur, former president Ulysses S. Grant, Grant's wife and a chief justice, who would all accompany them back to Washington. James A. Garfield would lie in state in the rotunda of the Capitol until he was moved and buried in Lakeview Cemetery in Cleveland.

Following the president's death, his doctors billed the federal government $91,000 for services rendered while attempting to save Garfield's life. And although this would be reduced to $27,500, their reputations would be damaged forever for having misjudged the location of the bullet and for the subsequent probing of their patient, which likely led to his blood infection. Charles Guiteau, who was sentenced to death and executed in June 1882, perhaps summed it up best when he was asked if he killed the president: "The doctors did that. I simply shot him."[50] At the age of forty-nine, James A. Garfield was the second president and the second youngest to be assassinated (John F. Kennedy would become the youngest in sixty years, being forty-six years old). His presidency lasted just two hundred days, yet for New Jersey, he left a long legacy. Others may have come and stayed, but only James Garfield became the commander in chief whose time in New Jersey would figure prominently in the story of his life and presidency.

Ironically, Garfield's death at the Jersey shore coincided with the beginning of some changes that would see an end of the Garden State, specifically Cape May and Long Branch, being the go-to vacation capital for U.S. executive officeholders. And although Garfield, Hayes and eventually Wilson would also visit the shore, the glamour the place exuberated in the middle of the nineteenth century would be all but gone by 1900. New Jersey historian Thomas Fleming wrote, "Garfield's death had cast a pall over Long Branch.

The influx of the sporting crowd had also soured many of the haughtier millionaires, and they began retreating to Saratoga and Newport."[51] By the time Benjamin Harrison spent some time in Long Branch during his single term in the late 1880s, the allure of the Jersey shore was in decline. Shortly before that, when Democrat Grover Cleveland, who was also born in New Jersey, won the presidency in 1884, he specifically avoided imitating his Republican predecessors in visiting the shore. Fleming said it best: "The Garden State's shore had become an ex-playground for presidents."[52]

The opulence of the Jersey Shore would evolve to become haven-like for middle-class Americans farther up the shoreline in Atlantic City, which would also alter the makeup of the formerly presidential shore towns. Most of the visitors were laboring people who flocked to the shore to rest and play by means of cheap train travel each Sunday from the 1870s through the twentieth century. And while the main excitement was reserved for Atlantic City, which had the nation's first boardwalk constructed in 1870, this new type of crowd also extended to Wildwood, Cape May and Long Branch.

After President Garfield's death in 1881, the tracks on which New Jersians had pushed his train cars to the seaside cottage were torn up. They were then purchased by one Oliver Byron, who then commissioned a local contractor to use the rails to construct a small structure that was forever to be known as the Garfield Tea House. The small structure is now owned by the Long Branch Historical Society and stands near the place where the Franklyn Cottage once stood. The ailing president's house, which he called home for the last twelve days of his life, was eventually torn down. Its site was ignored until the mid-twentieth century when the historical society dedicated a small stone memorial in Garfield's honor. In the president's eulogy, his secretary of state would memorialize his last days at the Jersey Shore: "Let us believe that in the silence of the receding world, he heard the great waves breaking on a further shore and felt already in his wasted brow the breath of eternal morning."[53]

4

THE THREE-CORNERED RACE OF TAFT, ROOSEVELT AND WILSON

T he election of 1912 was very contentious and memorable in the annals of American history. It is also the first one that really stood out for New Jersey. For one, it pitted a Garden State favorite, Theodore Roosevelt, against the incumbent, Howard Taft (the two men who collectively, with the late William McKinley, had made New Jersey a red state for the past four elections). But to make matters even more interesting, it brought into the fold the state's adopted son and then-current governor, Woodrow Wilson, for a truly New Jerseyan affair. The verdict for which way the state would swing hung in the air for months, making it a perfect microcosm of the national tension that kept voters agitated for months before November. By the summer of 1912, it was evident that New Jersey had become a battleground in an election that featured a then-current president, a former president, and the then-current head of the Garden State. The script hinted at drama, and it delivered.

THE THREE-CORNERED RACE FOR the presidency of the United States began on February 24, 1912. A jubilant and still massively popular Teddy Roosevelt proclaimed to have thrown his "hat in the ring," challenging his onetime friend and political successor, Howard Taft, for the Republican ticket. Having deflected the rumors that he was going to run for a third term, Roosevelt was persuaded to seek the nomination by a handful of progressive state governors

The official portrait of President William H. Taft from 1911, a year before he was forced to campaign to retain his party's nomination in the 1912 election. *Library of Congress.*

who asked him to put his objections to the idea aside for the betterment of the nation. Teddy accused the president of yielding to "the bosses and to the great privileged interests [being] disloyal to every canon of ordinary decency."[54] Yet Taft would not go down without a fight. Thus began the first-ever campaign by a current president in the primaries for the backing of his own party. "I am in this fight," he promised, "to perform a great public duty, the duty of keeping Theodore Roosevelt out of the White House."[55] Still, in the primary elections, which would see both men visit rambunctious New Jersey crowds, the winning total favored Teddy Roosevelt, who was declared a winner in nine of the twelve states that participated. But as evidenced in more modern elections, the pollsters do not always get it right.

Come June 12, 1912, at the Chicago Democratic Convention, Taft, having the floor, used his influence on party machinery to secure the Republican nomination. Even among the staunchest Republicans in Congress, there was no illusion that Taft would win. His sole purpose was to make sure that Roosevelt did not win and that the Republican Party could heal from the very apparent split caused by the former president. The fact was that many Republicans did not seem to agree with Roosevelt's reformist stance that catered to progressive ideas that were then rising from the local and state levels. The masses were beginning to look up to their federal government for an expanded role in ensuring people's welfare. The still mostly conservative Republican Party was not yet willing to yield to their demands. From the very beginning—and even more so then than ever—President Taft's conviction was to fight back against Roosevelt's challenge. "Even a rat," he explained, "will fight when driven into a corner."[56]

The fight got that much more complicated two weeks after the Republican convention in Chicago when members of both Democratic and Republican Parties who favored Roosevelt's progressivism reconvened in Chicago, formed the Progressive Party and nominated Roosevelt. The Progressive Party's platform called for, among other things, a minimum wage for women, an eight-hour workday, a social security system and a direct election of U.S. senators. The hope was that Roosevelt could steal the votes from Republicans and Democrats who had not yet chosen their man for the presidential ticket. The Democrats, on the other hand, saw things playing out in their favor. With the split in the Republican Party, they had to nominate a man who would satisfy the progressive aspects desired by the people without alienating the already left-leaning party. The Democratic camp needed its own progressive candidate. And it just so happened that the perfect man for the job was right there, waiting for them in New Jersey.

In two short years as governor, the Virginia-born onetime Princeton professor Woodrow Wilson had already established himself as a major progressive, able to push through most of the reforms that the progressives of both the Democratic and Republican Parties had failed to accomplish in twenty years leading up to his election. New Jersey's population soared to 2,537,167 in 1910, manufacturing had doubled since the beginning of the century and taxable property had tripled in value; progressive legislation was desperately needed for the urban state.[57] Wilson's election in 1910 was a repudiation of the party boss politics and laissez-faire Republicanism that favored the business owners at the cost of the ever-growing working class. Once in power, Wilson turned his administration's attention to reforming elections, passing a corruption practices act, creating a strong public utility commission and signing a workmen's compensation act.[58]

Wilson would spend months at a time in 1911 at speaking engagements away from Trenton. It was evident that his eyes were turned toward the White House. Wilson's public views on the nation's course were collectively labeled as the "New Freedom," which countered Roosevelt's insistence on regulating big business with the direct government action of breaking down monopolies and restoring freedom of competition. Wilson secured the Democratic nomination on the forty-sixth ballot through the shrewdness of his managers swaying southern loyalists to recognize his Virginia roots and the progressive Democrats to see his progressive New Jersey reforms. The stage was set by July 1912.

The was no denying the fact that the Garden State became the battleground between the leading candidates, who competed in courting each other's supporters. The final race to the White House began in early August 1912. While Teddy Roosevelt chose the Progressive convention in Chicago, full of speeches kickstarted by Progressive darling Robert LaFollette, denunciations of Democrats and personal attacks against Taft, Wilson opened more calmly at the summer residence of New Jersey governors in Sea Grit. For the first

LONG BRANCH DAILY RECORD

LONG BRANCH, N. J., MONDAY, NOVEMBER 4, 1912.

PULPIT SPEAKS FOR SUNDAY ORDINANCE

Preachers Urge Voters to Back Up Commissioners on Ordinance Referendum.

GOVERNOR WILSON RECEIVES WARM MONMOUTH GREETING; PRAISES SCULLY AND TAYLOR

Halls Taxed Beyond Capacity Here and at Red Bank to Hear Presidential Candidate, Who Expressed Confidence In Winning and Makes Plea For Democratic House and Senate.

CHATTLE GRADUATE ON VARSITY SQUAD

Leroy Throckmorton, Class 1910, Subject of Fine Write up at Syracuse, N. Y.

WOODROW WILSON.

100 ELKS VISIT

New Jersey governor Woodrow Wilson did not campaign much in New Jersey until the last few weeks before the 1912 election. He initially believed that his tenure as the state's governor was enough to convince New Jerseyans that he was the man for the national job. Long Branch *(NJ)* Daily Record, *November 4, 1912.*

time, the eyes of the nation were on the Garden State, eagerly awaiting the drama that was about to unfold in the upcoming presidential election. In fact, Wilson would almost ensure that was the case by remaining in his role and even stepping up his pace as governor in Trenton in the last weeks of his campaign and eventually while awaiting his inauguration. He would not step down from his governor's post until four days before being sworn in as president of the United States. During his last days as the head of the state, the president-elect even persuaded the state legislature to pass seven laws abolishing most of the privileges of giant trusts—a progressive until the end.[59]

NEW JERSEY BECAME THE benefactor of the political turmoil caused by Teddy Roosevelt in early 1912. Months before he went off to represent the Progressive Party, Teddy Roosevelt ceremoniously announced that he would be willing to accept the Republican nomination, concurrently defying his self-appointed successor and onetime ally, William H. Taft. With the state firmly in the Republicans' grasp since the late nineteenth century and with a high percentage of the population voting red, the fight for the Republican nomination needed to take on the fervor generally reserved for the presidential election itself. The weekend of May 24, 1912, proved to be extremely busy, as all three presidential candidates for the Republican ticket whirled through the state almost simultaneously. The eyes of the world were on New Jersey, and if one were judging the outcome of the race by the reception awarded to the three men in the Garden State, it was clear that this would indeed be a very contentious election.

The first presidential candidate to arrive in the state was Wisconsin senator Robert M. LaFollette. Ironically, his lackluster reception in Jersey, together with the large crowds that turned out for his opponents, convinced the progressive politician to withdraw from contention within mere weeks of his visit. Initially, a guest at a luncheon in Asbury Park on Friday, the senator gave his first speech at the Savoy Theatre. And although he was introduced by the mayor, LaFollette's speech was heard by only a handful of spectators who could not even fill all the available theater seats. The situation did not get much better when he arrived at his main event at the Long Branch train station, where a crowd of barely five hundred citizens greeted him. The Long Branch's *Daily Record* described the senator's voice as being hoarse and barely audible over the arriving and departing trains. LaFollette attacked both Roosevelt and Taft for failing to enforce the Sherman Law, which, if adequately followed, would have prevented the growth of monopolies, which he claimed were responsible for the plight of the working people.[60] Yet while looking out into the dwindling audience, even Lafollette, the model of progressive reform on the state level, could see the writing on the wall. As he spoke, some members in the back of the crowd began to slowly turn their backs and quietly walk away.

President William Howard Taft opened his New Jersey campaign on Friday, May 24, 1912, in Camden, New Jersey, where he spoke listlessly on the strife between himself and his former boss, Teddy Roosevelt.

"Thousands Honored Nation's Chief Upon His First Visit to Camden Last Night," proclaimed the *Camden Daily Courier*. The president received a very affectionate reception, which the newspapers announced would be "long remembered, not only by his admirers but by the general citizenship because of the fact that not the slightest untoward event occurred to mark the evening and because of the absence of displays of rowdyism so often noted at monster political gatherings."[61] It was noted by everyone present that Taft's agenda was one of a defensive nature, a response to the vitriolic attacks on his presidency by his onetime boss. The keynote of his speech was the fact that allowing him a second term at the helm was as crucial to his fulfillment of his campaign promises and the preservation of a constitutional government. "If you give Roosevelt a third term, there is no reason why he should not demand and get a fourth....Then all the barriers are down," stated the president, clearly elated by the turnout and support.[62]

The president left the cheering Camden crowds and boarded the train to nearby Burlington. He then moved on to his main event at the Trenton State Armory, assisted by United States senator Frank O. Briggs, Quartermaster General C. Edward Murray and several secret service agents. His trek through the city streets of Trenton was cheered on by rows of thousands of people (around eight thousand, to be precise). When the procession of cars reached the armory where Taft would give the main speech of his New Jersey campaign stop, crowds yelled his name, and little kids perched on their fathers' shoulders waved their caps. Inside the gallery, cheers and noise that seemed to threaten the very foundation of the building's structure greeted the president. "As he glanced around the galleries dilled with ladies and children, every one of whom carried a tiny American flag," reported one newspaper editorial, "a broad smile spread itself across the features of the candidate for the Republican nomination."[63]

When it was time for him to speak, Taft made his way to the podium and, owing to the cheering and shouting of the crowd, was unable to begin for a few minutes until the excitement subsided. "I regret the necessity that brings me out. I feel humiliated that I, as president of the United States, am the first one that has had to depart from the traditions that keep the president at home during political controversy."[64] He then appealed for the support of New Jersey voters based on his administration's record of having eliminated more trusts than the previous Roosevelt administration. He also spoke at length about opposing Mr. Roosevelt's mudslinging campaign that he was waging against Taft. He then attacked Roosevelt's misinterpretation of information and facts to suit his narrative. He also had choice words to say against Roosevelt breaking the tradition of not running for a third term, a precedent that dated to George Washington's presidency. Taft finished his speech by stating that it would be a sad day in the nation's history if they had to depend on one man for existence. Nobody was more significant than the government of the people and by the people, not even Teddy Roosevelt. Taft waved his big hand and somberly left the stage as the room erupted in cheer.

After spending the night as a guest of General Murray, the president resumed his itinerary the next morning, traveling to the northern portions of New Jersey. He delivered the same message, with notable stops in Montclair, Rutherford, Englewood, Hackensack, Fort Lee, Ridgewood and Lodi. In many of these places, he spoke from the back of his automobile. In Ridgewood, the reporters proclaimed that he was greeted by the largest gathering ever reported in the town's history. Notified of the elaborate preparations being made for his stop, Taft obliged and pledged to speak for ten minutes. As there was no auditorium in Ridgewood large enough to accommodate the number of people who wished to hear him, the president gave his message of hope in preserving the integrity of the executive office from the porch of a country club. After extending his greeting to the masses, he looked over the golf course and exclaimed that he would rather be out there enjoying a game than discussing the political situation. After his ten-minute speech, the local Boy Scouts saluted the departing president as a band's drums and bugles played in the background. The Rutherford Taft League prepared its city auditorium for Taft's arrival at the next stop. He followed the city mayor and other local officials to the stage with a shorter version of his last speech. The president, however, took a lot longer to speak to the people outside, where he stood in his open-top automobile at the depot square and delivered a nearly quarter-hour-long address to the cheering crowds.

Although each of these towns threw galas and specialized events surrounding the arrival of the president, Taft was never really anywhere long enough for him to appreciate it. His May 25, 1912 itinerary in Bergen County was very tight, with Ridgewood scheduled for late in the afternoon, followed by Rutherford at 9:05 p.m., Lodi at 9:20 p.m., and Hackensack at 9:35 p.m.; then to Englewood until 10:40 p.m.; then to Fort Lee at 11:00 p.m. at Cella's hotel; and then to Edgewater at 11:30 p.m., before leaving via a special ferry boat for New York at 12:00 a.m.[65] Undoubtedly the largest stop of the day occurred in Paterson that very morning. Ten thousand people came to hear Taft speak at the city's armory. "I now present you the president of the United States. God grant that he be president for four years more!"[66] Those present recalled the cheers and applause that followed as deafening, the colorful crowd waving red, white, and blue handkerchiefs. A smiling president waved his arms and thanked his audience before starting his speech.

He was very straightforward in expressing his views about the personal attacks of his biggest opponent. The masses applauded and cheered on every criticism he made of Roosevelt. Frequently, Taft found it necessary to lift his hand in an appeal to the audience to desist from applauding in order to save time, as he had many more meetings to attend in Bergen County that afternoon.[67] The entire speech lasted twenty minutes, with Taft asking those present who could not stay for its entirety to leave before he started speaking—nobody took him up on his suggestion. The speech itself was, word for word, the same speech he had given the night prior in Camden, and it was reprinted in its entirety in Paterson's *Morning Call* newspaper two days later. The newspaper proudly proclaimed that the visit and reception had been "more enthusiastic than the one at which Roosevelt spoke on [a couple of days prior], and it far surpassed the La Follette meeting of Friday night." While Roosevelt was perhaps a more popular Republican candidate and personality, Taft was still the president of the United States. His visit was an honor and an occasion. With the divisive politics of the twenty-first century, it may be hard to imagine that in 1912, the masses who turned out to see the presidents did not count themselves as Republican, Democratic or even Progressive. They were citizens of the United States who came out to see their commander in chief.

William Taft's visit to New Jersey came on the heels of Theodore Roosevelt's very own excursion into the Garden State just days before. The former president's itinerary did not differ much from Taft's, as his stops alongside heavily Republican towns coincided with the stops the president would make within twenty-four hours. The major difference between Roosevelt's stops and those of his successor dealt much with the dichotomy of their personalities. While Taft remained very proper and reserved, always sticking to the script, the rambunctious Roosevelt was not afraid to walk into the crowd and shake hands with his fans, who were reportedly mostly women. He was a true celebrity, and hence, his appearances had more of a sensationalized feel than the more formal Taft appearances. One newspaper reported, "It was impossible to tell…from the attitude of the audience whether or not the interest was manifested because they were looking up at the most talked about man in the world, or whether they were straining to catch the [presidential nominee's] voice."[68]

Former president Theodore Roosevelt speaking to New Jerseyans during his 1912 Republican primaries tour of the Garden State. *Library of Congress.*

After making his way from South New Jersey up to Morris, Bergen, and Essex Counties, Roosevelt drew his largest crowds in Paterson, Passaic, and Newark, all nearing ten thousand spectators. This did not mean that he did not have his share of welcomes in the smaller towns, such as Rutherford and Lodi. In the latter, all the buildings along Main Street were draped in red, white, and blue, with a "beautifully decorated" speaker stand erected in front of the First National Bank Building. It did not matter that the former president would only have ten minutes to speak. In anticipation of Roosevelt's arrival, the town marshals, the entire fire department, and the police were equipped with clubs and ordered to keep the peace and handle the crowds. Thirty minutes before his 3:00 p.m. scheduled arrival, all the public school students, led by the school bands, marched down Main Street. Out of the nearly one thousand students, half of them attended the Roosevelt School. Carrying flags, the kids arranged themselves between the street and the speaker stand.

When Roosevelt arrived, loud cheers broke the restless murmurs, especially after he stood up in his open-top automobile and waved his hat. The former president mounted the platform to the cheers of the approximately five thousand spectators and began his unscripted eight-minute talk: "I am very glad to be here and to see all these children. They will be our future citizens." He then went into discussing his policies by prefacing, "I want to see these children grow up with a fair chance for an education and to give them a fair chance to earn a livelihood so they can, by honest and industrious labor, have a full dinner pail and something to spare." The crowd erupted in cheers that took a full minute to calm down. Roosevelt then went on to finish his speech. His address ended in a very similar fashion as all his others did; he went near the crowd and shook hands before departing for his next stops in Rutherford and Hackensack. At one point, after Roosevelt got in his car, there was some commotion coming from the multitude of vehicles of spectators that blocked the road. Roosevelt calmly leaned over to Lodi's police chief and informed him that he used to be a police commissioner and that he could help him untangle things. The chief laughed at the suggestion and simply ordered Roosevelt's motorcade to go around the tangled cars.

Teddy Roosevelt was forced to stop his vehicle on many occasions to please the crowds of people who came out to see him as he made his way through New Jersey in 1912. *Library of Congress.*

As the twenty or so vehicles full of the former president's entourage and the media were driving away, Roosevelt spotted two old ladies waving small American flags. In a very chivalrous fashion, the onetime colonel ordered the car to stop, and he jumped out and vigorously shook the ladies' hands. "The colonel is a wise campaigner," wrote the *Passaic Daily News*. "He never missed a trick with the women, and they seemed all to be for him."[69] Everywhere the cars went, a shower of Roosevelt buttons followed from the entourage, and as kids climbed over the adults to get their hands on them.

There seemed to be no end to cheering crowds as the motorcade made its way through Garfield, Hackensack, Hasbrouck Heights, Woodbridge and Rutherford. All off the cuff, Roosevelt's speeches were very similar in pushing forth his progressive agenda. As the auto parade kicked up a significant amount of dust on the still-to-be paved roadways, newspapers reported that Roosevelt's face was dirty, and his collar was witted when the former president reached Hasbrouck Heights. There, Roosevelt spoke laughingly to the detachment of Boys Scouts standing near his podium. "I hope you'll vote as you shout on Tuesday!" A distinctively female ripple of cheers and laughter was said to have erupted at the comment.[70] It was in Hackensack that Roosevelt praised New Jersey directly: "I thoroughly enjoyed the trip through New Jersey," he said. "I've had some middling lively times in the West, but New Jersey put one over the West. I've passed about a strenuous ten hours as I ever had in my life, but I've been pleasured all the way!"[71] Teddy paused his speech in Rutherford as he waited for one of the local politicians to go to a nearby store to get him a lemon soda. As he closed his remarks and got back into his car, Roosevelt extended his hand and shook hands with dozens of his supporters. His next engagement made for a humorous scene in Woodridge. Many school personnel lined up in front of the schoolhouse, hoping that the former president, even though he was running late, would stop and say a few words. All they got was Roosevelt's big smile and a wave of a hat in his hand as his car continued on its way.

There was one stop on Roosevelt's New Jersey tour that perhaps foreshadowed his limitations as the undisputed man of the people. During his visit to Paterson, where ten thousand men and women came to hear him speak, the charisma that had made him one of the most popular personalities in the world had somehow run out of steam. "Standing out above everything else at the Fifth Regiment Armory yesterday noon," proclaimed Paterson's *Morning Call*, "was the apparent lack of enthusiasm that manifested itself in the audience toward Theodore Roosevelt, candidate for president of the United States."[72] The biggest knock against Roosevelt seemed to be the fact

The crowds could not get enough of the former president Teddy Roosevelt when he stumped though New Jersey. He is pictured here in Paterson, New Jersey. *Library of Congress.*

that his orator skills were very overexaggerated. His voice could not be heard by nearly half of those in the audience. At times, when applause would have been more appropriate, the quietness made for some awkward moments. Speaking for forty-five minutes, Roosevelt appeared to have directed his full attention toward the staff of journalists and photographers who took up the platform to the right of him. "His speech was in measure, a disappointment to the thousands who expected him to deliver one of his famous 'punch' speeches," noted one editorial.[73] And although the audience warmed up a bit toward the end of the speech, when Teddy made his last remarks, there were only a few spontaneous cheers instead of the usual spontaneous outburst from the crowd.

The *Hackensack Evening Record* concurred with the *Morning Call*'s assertion that the former president failed to make a real statement for his candidacy. The thousands who came out to see Theodore Roosevelt came not so much to see a man running for president but to witness a former commander in chief, and with that in mind, the reception was very much in line with what one was to expect when a president comes to town. In Hackensack, the local journalists labeled half the crowd that observed the speech in the armory as women and children and the other half as Democrats. The editorial agreed that people came out not for a candidate but for "a spectacular individual and because he is an ex-president."[74] The local Republican committee went on record to say that Roosevelt did not create the impression expected from his visit. "His speech at the armory was devoid of any special interest and did not arouse any enthusiasm," proclaimed one local legislator. "His speech was not half interesting or instructive," commented another.[75]

Teddy Roosevelt greets the people of Paterson, New Jersey, during his tour of the state in 1912. *Library of Congress.*

Although Wilson was the New Jersey connection to this election, he was still merely a governor, not a former or then-current president like his opponents. As such, his campaign does not necessarily fit the narrative presented by Taft or Roosevelt. Ironically, while his connection to New Jersey made the visits of the other candidates quite a big deal, Wilson himself downplayed his campaigning in the state. In a statement to the Garden State voters, the future president proclaimed that it was unnecessary for him to take the stump to enforce his candidacy. He preferred instead to leave his record as governor as his best argument and the source of the opposition as his only explanation of why there should be any campaign at all in New Jersey.[76] At least one editorial agreed with this assertion when Asbury Park Press editor J.L. Kinmonth stated, "The governor was quite within his privilege to make himself known to the voters in other sections of the country, but in New Jersey, he needs no other laudation than the memory of his deeds."[77] None of this stopped the governor from printing public appeals to New Jersey voters to support him at the polls, especially for the Democratic nomination. Yet Wilson did not spend a single moment campaigning in his adopted home state.

After Taft received the Republican Party's endorsement and Roosevelt announced his plans to run on a third party ticket, it was time for Wilson to pick up his appearances across the state. Embarking on a missive stump tour two weeks before election day, the New Jersey governor spoke at no less

Left: Theodore Roosevelt speaking to New Jersey crowds. *Library of Congress.*

Below: A picture of President Woodrow Wilson in Princeton, New Jersey, where he went to cast a vote in favor of the Women's Suffrage Amendment on October 19, 1915. *Library of Congress.*

than one hundred meetings. "And although it has lacked much of the glitter of marching demonstrations that have marked the presidential campaigns [of his opponents]," proclaimed the *Passaic Daily Journal*, "the present has been one of the most strenuous out of all the candidates."[78] Still, these were not visits from the president of the United States, so they did not have the same exhilaration. When he stopped in Long Branch in Monmouth County, Wilson was greeted by 1,200 people, what the *Long Branch Daily Record* called "a great crowd." In nearby Red Bank on November 4, 1912, the last leg of

Woodrow Wilson's summer home in Sea Grit, New Jersey. He would run his 1912 and 1916 campaigns from its porch. *Library of Congress.*

President Woodrow Wilson acknowledging his Democratic nomination for the presidency. The event took place at Shadow Lawn, the "summer White House," near Long Branch, New Jersey, in 1916. *Library of Congress.*

the tour, 2,000 men and women came out to hear him speak. In Middletown Township, the crowds shrunk to slightly below 800. "The fate of New Jersey depends on the election Tuesday," bellowed the future president. "Do you want the government to slip back to the interest [of those] who practically owned this state and the nation?"[79]

All the intensely packed stumping in the campaign's waning days led to one of the more interesting incidents of Wilson's push for the presidency. While traveling back from Red Bank at high speeds to make the next appointment, the governor's limousine was near Hightstown when it got into an accident that left Wilson concussed and bleeding. According to the reports, there was a mount in the road left by a recent excavation, and due to the slight shadow caused by a telephone pole, the driver did not see it, striking the obstruction. Wilson was jolted from his seat and hit his head on the roof of the car. The driver decided to take the president to the home of the nearest physician. A local man, Dr. Titus, was routed out of bed; he then shaved off a fair patch of the governor's hair and bandaged the three-inch gash.[80] Luckily, the only destination left on the trail was the governor's home in Princeton, twelve miles away, and this time, the driver took a more leisurely pace.

WHEN ALL WAS SAID and done, the respective vigor that met each of the three respective campaigners in New Jersey foreshadowed the election's outcome. As predicted, Roosevelt's choice to run on a third-party ticket split the Republican Party and gave the presidency to the least popular of the three candidates, Woodrow Wilson. The crowds in New Jersey towns did not lie. Wilson might have won, but he did so without winning the majority of the votes. Nationally, he received 6,296,547 to 4,188,571 for Roosevelt and 3,486,720 for Taft. In New Jersey, which gave Wilson its fourteen electoral votes, he received only 178,189 votes out of 462,289 cast, a mere 38 percent alongside the 42 percent he received nationally.[81] He then had a bigger headache to look forward to, the office of the president of the United States.

5

THE ALLURE OF FRANKLIN D. ROOSEVELT

T he election of 1936 is undisputedly the textbook definition of a presidential election landslide, and much of this can be attributed to the allure of one man, Franklin Delano Roosevelt. And this affliction that had not escaped the people of New Jersey. "There is one issue in this campaign," Roosevelt told one of his advisors in early 1936, "It's myself, and people must be either for me or against me."[82] As conceited as the statement must have seemed to those around Roosevelt when he said it, there would certainly not be too many people who would argue with its merit.

Roosevelt became the president of the United States in 1932, after a dismal four years under Herbert Hoover. He would become synonymous with his relief, reform, and recovery programs, collectively known as the New Deal. And although his measures by no means brought back the prosperity of the Roaring 1920s, they did pull the nation out of malaise by making the people's lives generally a little better than they were under Roosevelt's predecessor. Simultaneously, it made Roosevelt a downright hero—the man the public heard on the radio through his weekly fireside chats, saw on the front covers of newspapers and felt each time they picked up a check from a relief agency or a New Deal–sponsored job. And although he was very polarizing with his overreach of executive power in creating many of the reforms that would later be seen as unconstitutional to the American people, he was the celebrity of his time. With the unprecedented popularity of his wife and first lady, Eleanor Roosevelt, the American president was unstoppable in his bid for reelection. The reception awarded to the Roosevelts in their multiple visits

President Franklin D. Roosevelt in 1936. *Library of Congress.*

to the Garden State in late 1936 certainly denoted their national popularity. There was no surprise at the polls that November when Roosevelt won 523 electoral votes to his opponent's 8.

With its many industries scattered across the state, New Jersey was hit hard by the onset of the Great Depression following the October 1929 stock market crash. The situation only worsened in the years that followed under the guidance of President Herbert Hoover. And while it would be unfair to blame the economic downturn on Hoover, his insistence on rugged individualism and self-help and steadfast belief in a laissez-faire government without much business regulation led to the situation on Main Streets across America significantly worsening. By 1930, the copper refineries of Middlesex County, Camden's shipyards and the iron mines of Dover and Ringwood had all closed their doors. Similarly, by the end of the same year, the textile mills of Paterson and Passaic and the highly diversified industries of Newark, where more than 7,500 families were already on relief, were shut down.[83] In Morris and Somerset Counties, millionaires shuttered their mansions and estates, laying off countless maids, cooks and gardeners. The economy had plummeted, and New Jerseyans were feeling the pain like their neighbors across the nation. The average annual personal income in New Jersey in 1929 was $839; it dipped to $479 in 1932 and further to $433 a year later.[84]

When Franklin Delano Roosevelt was inaugurated as president on March 4, 1933, the nation seemed to be mourning, losing the fight against the dissipating American dream. More than 40 percent of New Jersey banks had gone out of business, taking all of their clients' life savings with them.

President Herbert Hoover during a brief 1932 stop in Newark, New Jersey. *Joseph Bilby.*

Bread lines that wrapped around entire city blocks were commonplace, as were the sights of men and women selling apples on street corners for pennies a day and homeless individuals roaming the countryside seeking any possible work. There was a lot of hope for the man who had taken over the mantle of the American presidency, the one who promised the American people that the only thing they had to fear was fear itself. By 1933, more than thirteen million men and women were unemployed, countless towns faced bankruptcy, and people roamed the streets looking for work while others ate out of garbage pails.[85]

The new president began waging his war against the Great Depression right away. He started by closing and then reopening all of the nation's banks under better supervision. His administration then created a plethora of work programs to get money once again flowing into the American people's pockets. In the process, he would endear himself in the hearts of his people. In what became known as "Roosevelt's first hundred days," the new Democratic president introduced new legislation that was designed to rapidly put Americans back to work. The success of the Civilian Conservation Corps (CCC) in the Garden State foreshadowed what New Jerseyans could expect from Washington. The CCC employed young men between the ages of seventeen and twenty-five for up to a year to perform construction and conservation work, all while paying them thirty dollars a month, twenty-five dollars of which was sent back to their families at home. Camps were set up all across the state, with the young men assisting in reforestation and tree planting along the cliffs of the Palisades and the marshes of Hackensack Valley, as well as High Point State Park in Sussex County, to name a few.[86]

Roosevelt's New Deal was at work across the nation through the Works Progress Administration (WPA), one of the more successful relief programs, which employed 3.5 million people. By the election of 1936, more than 100,000 New Jersey men and women were employed by the WPA.[87] They improved parks, built post offices and public schools where there were none, and dug mosquito ditches in swamplands. Apart from many other noteworthy projects, the WPA workers of New Jersey also built the Roosevelt Stadium in Jersey City, constructed the Bacharach Home for infantile paralysis victims in Atlantic City, built a Greek amphitheater at Montclair State College and restored and built the Grover Cleveland House in Caldwell and Speedwell Park in Morristown.[88] In seven years, the WPA built more than six thousand miles of streets and highways in New Jersey. It constructed 326 new bridges, repaired 324 others and built or improved more than 4,000 culverts under highways. Behind it all, the people of New Jersey saw not the program but the man. Regardless of whether one agreed with his overextension of the federal government in providing direct aid to the people, there was no denying the fact that although the Depression was far from over, fear was giving way to hope under the presidency of Franklin D. Roosevelt.

The New Deal rolled along into 1936 when the man at the helm of it all visited the state. He received an unprecedented reception from hundreds of thousands of spectators. Things were looking up for the people of the Garden State. When the president pushed for the repeal of the Eighteenth Amendment, ending Prohibition in April 1933, breweries and winemakers across the state went on a hiring spree. And of course, this also played a prominent role in raising the spirits of beleaguered Americans. Salaries continued to be low during the New Deal years, but jobs kept coming. The weekly paycheck also mattered less when it could be offset by admissions to movies for twenty-five cents, full course dinners for fifty cents, gasoline for ten to twelve cents a gallon and food budgets for newlyweds of eight or nine dollars a week.[89] Thus, on the eve of his reelection in 1936, Roosevelt was riding high in the Garden State, a true celebrity president. The clearest point of reference for the people of the nation and the state in 1936, expressed by historian Walter LaFeber, was the year 1932: "Any inadequacies of Roosevelt's policies, when compared with those of Hoover, did not seem so great after all."[90] While visiting the state in 1932 as a candidate for the nation's highest office, Roosevelt received a modest yet forgettable reception at Sea Grit. When he came back to the state in October 1936, this time as the president of the United States and the man who, in the eyes of many, was the champion who pulled them out of the Great Depression, his reception was much less forgettable.

IT WOULD BE IMPOSSIBLE not to place Roosevelt's visit to New Jersey on October 2, 1936, in the context of Jersey City mayor Frank Hague's political "organization." As the chairman of the Democratic National Committee for much of the early twentieth century, Hague is often referred to by historians as the "granddaddy of Jersey bosses."[91] During the pinnacle of his power, his "organization," as it was known by the press, controlled much of the Garden State's politics and even extended its influence to the national political arena. At the time of his death, *TIME* magazine estimated Hague's wealth was more than $10 million on a salary of less than $9,000 a year. Ironically, the party boss chose to endorse Roosevelt's opponent for the Democratic ticket in 1932, something he would have to rectify come reelection time. Infamously known for his use of voter fraud and demand for uncompromising loyalty from his constituents, once Roosevelt got the Democratic nomination in 1932, Hague quickly readjusted his allegiance and promised to support Roosevelt going forward. That is not to say that Franklin's elections were fraudulent. Yet it does bring awareness to Hague's political power concerning state and national politics. Crossing Hague would have been near political suicide for any Democrat, even one with the last name of Roosevelt. At the request of the Jersey City mayor, the president officially opened his first-ever campaign for president in New Jersey back in 1932 and then returned in 1936.

President Franklin Delano Roosevelt visited Jersey City on October 2, 1936, once again as a favor to Hague's political machine. This time, the commander in chief dedicated a massive medical complex building in Hague's city, and it was incidentally built through federal funding approved by the president. The maternity ward of the new building would be named after the mayor's mother, Margaret Hague. Although Jersey City was not

Franklin D. Roosevelt with Jersey City mayor Frank Hague during his 1932 campaign stop in Sea Grit, New Jersey. *Joseph Bilby.*

billed as a campaign stop, there was no denying that it was the impetus for garnering good publicity on the eve of Roosevelt's imminent reelection. And in the Garden State, Hague would be the one to help deliver it in one of the most, if not the most, exuberant presidential stops in the state's history.

The Hague Show, as some newspapers dubbed Roosevelt's October 2 visit, had cost $10,000, about $200,000 today. The *Chicago Tribune* wrote, "Mayor Hague, Democratic political boss of Jersey City, grasped the opportunity to put on a show that left members of the presidential party gasping—a superb exhibition of political efficiency."[92] On the afternoon of Roosevelt's arrival in Jersey City, seventy thousand school children stood on each side of the road as the president traveled on to the dedication. They all held American flags and wore red, white, and blue paper caps with dedicated sashes draped across their chests. When Roosevelt's open-top car slowly rolled down the street, photographers snapped pictures of the smiling president as he applauded the thousands of students chanting, "We want Roosevelt!" Hague had declared the occasion a civic holiday and a day off, a paid one at that, and the move paid dividends. Every street from the Holland Tunnel route to Roosevelt's speaking engagement at the Jersey City Medical Center was

Franklin D. Roosevelt with Jersey City mayor Frank Hague on his right, speaking at a campaign stop in 1932 in Sea Girt, New Jersey. *Joseph Bilby.*

draped in Roosevelt banners. Seemingly every building was covered with pinned-up posters of his likeness.

According to newspaper reports across the nation, 250,000 Jerseyans cheered the Democratic president as he mounted the temporary stage to speak. After a brief but elaborate fireworks display, Hague introduced Roosevelt to an arousing display of support. "We of Jersey City worship and honor the name, Roosevelt!" In "the President's wildest and noisiest demonstration of his career," the crowd went wild after his introduction.[93] After returning the mayor's compliment and proclaiming that the city should be proud of having a leader such as Hague, Roosevelt reminded the people that what they saw in the massive medical building was the New Deal at work: "I am happy that the federal government, through its public works expenditures, has been able to be of assistance to the municipal government of Jersey City in making this center possible."[94] "Assisting" was an understatement. The federal aid given to Hudson County alone amounted to $1,760,343 in grants and $4,069,400 in loans in 1933 and $3,831,136 in grants and $2,430,000 in loans two years later.

President Roosevelt dedicated Jersey City's twenty-one-story medical center. The following spread appeared in a New Brunswick newspaper. *Top*: President Franklin D. Roosevelt at the dedication with Mayor Frank Hague (*left*) of Jersey City and Colonel E.M. Watson, his military aid. *Bottom*: a part of the more than two-hundred-thousand-person crowd that greeted the president. Daily Home News *(New Brunswick, NJ), October 3, 1936.*

Roosevelt did not stay long in New Jersey that day. In fact, he left shortly after arriving and giving his speech in Jersey City. As much of a spectacle as his visit turned out to be, the fate of his reelection still seemed up in the air when it came to the Garden State. There was no hiding the statistic that while he might have won the state's vote in 1932, the people of New Jersey had not given a majority of their votes to a Democratic candidate since

1892. The state's Republican lean was evident in Roosevelt's first election, which he only won by a narrow margin of 49.5 percent of the vote to Herbert Hoover's 47.6 percent.[95] Perhaps these numbers brought the president back to New Jersey once again a week before the 1936 election against Kansas governor Alf Landon. The latter, who is now lost to New Jersey history, had numerous stops in the Garden State himself. Before departing for nearby New York City on October 28, Landon addressed the Newark City crowd of around six thousand. He spoke of protecting U.S. labor and separating it from the clutches of corrupt politics. His visit to the state's Republican stronghold paled in comparison to his opponent's stump campaign through the Garden State, which began the same day with a visit to Bayonne, New Jersey.

The main impetus for Roosevelt's October 28 stop in the tristate area of New York, New Jersey, and Connecticut was the rededication of the Statue of Liberty, nested on Liberty Island in New York Harbor between the shores of both New York and New Jersey. He would finish the stump that day by praising the nation's settlers for their love of freedom and then promising the American people that "we shall continue to build an even better home for liberty."[96] Yet before the big New York event, which drew all the prominent newspaper journalists and radio announcers, the day began as a big deal for New Jersey's Bayonne citizens. The president's train arrived at the New Jersey station from Washington at 9:30 a.m. There, ten thousand people welcomed it. Roosevelt would not stay more than twenty minutes in the Garden State that day before departing for New York by automobile, yet he specifically chose to make New Jersey the starting point of his trip, even though he could have gone directly to the Big Apple. He knew the importance of speaking, albeit briefly, to the crowds of roughly thirty thousand people who lined the Bayonne streets to greet him. As he appeared on the platform wearing his light felt hat and waving his hands to the crowd, a band played "Happy Days Are Here Again."

After going to his waiting vehicle, the president was first introduced by Mayor Lucious Donohoe and then by the man who unofficially ruled the state's political arena, Jersey City mayor Frank Hague. A smiling Roosevelt spoke briefly. "I am glad to come back here and glad your factories and industrial plants are running again." He pointed out that there was greater security and prosperity in the nation since his previous visit to the area in 1932 when he was still just another politician seeking the Democratic nomination. He said it was "the kind of prosperity which will last the people through their lives and those of their children."[97] What made the short stop that much

Franklin D. Roosevelt and Eleanor Roosevelt at the 1933 inauguration. It was the first of four inaugurations he would preside over as president of the United States. *Library of Congress.*

more of a media highlight was the fact that Mrs. Roosevelt had come from New York to meet her husband at the Bayonne station, and she also spoke a few words before the arrival of her husband. A local senator introduced her as the wife of "the greatest president we've had since Abraham Lincoln." As the auto procession left the station for the Bayonne-Staten Island Bridge through the massive wildly cheering crowds that lined the streets, a band began playing "Auld Lang Syne," a popular song often sung as a farewell or ending of big celebrations. Looking up from his open-top car, President and Eleanor Roosevelt could hardly miss the giant sign on a building opposite the station. "Welcome to our city, Mr. President. In 1932, Bayonne gave you a majority of 16,568. In 1936, you will receive a majority of over 20,000. Bayonne City Democratic Committee."[98]

Two days later, on October 30, the American president had a much more official stump visit in New Jersey's Camden, where he presided over the dedication of a park that would come to bear his name. The Roosevelt hype train kicked into high gear, for lack of a better term. The celebrity president and his wife were cheered on by a "record ovation" of one hundred thousand people who came out to see the most famous man in the nation. Fifty thousand jammed into the new Roosevelt Plaza in front of city hall, and as many more lined the streets to hear him give a campaign speech. The *Camden Evening Courier* was blunt with its opinion of the visit: "Camden has never seen anything like it and probably never will again. It was a demonstration of loyalty that must have warmed the president's great heart."[99] This was truly quite a display of love for the president, who arrived in Camden nearly forty minutes late, as he was kept by the five hundred thousand Philadelphians who had come out to hear him speak that morning in Pennsylvania. His car could only average eight miles per hour as it made its way from Pennsylvania to Camden, as masses of people had to be moved out of the way by local police enforcement. Shocked by the outpouring of support, Roosevelt remarked to his secretary, "This [is] the greatest thing I ever saw in my life."[100]

The crowds in Camden waited patiently to see their president. Music and a plethora of preplanned speeches kept at least those near the platform at the plaza entertained for hours leading up to the president's late arrival. Once again, one of the people who warmed up the crowd was Frank Hague, who proclaimed the president's victory the following week. "You people in Camden hold the line," he said, "and North Jersey will put him over." He was followed by local radio entertainers who led the between-speech singing until they were interrupted by the noise of an airplane flying low above the crowds of people, a sign attached to its tail, "Mr. President, Philadelphia is yours!" The crowd below erupted with, "So is Camden!" On the stage, one of the entertainers bellowed into the microphone, "Who is Camden for?" The answer came back in a deafening roar: "Roosevelt!"[101]

The elation for the president's visit had started much earlier than the 5:00 p.m. time when he actually showed up to speak. All day, thousands of men and women marched from their industrial plants, drove in from the suburbs, and met at their designated spots near the newly named Roosevelt Plaza. Newspapers reported that people were climbing to housetops and leaning from open windows to look for the presidential party arriving from Philadelphia. At the approaches to Camden Bridge, people climbed along the walkovers and hung over the sides to get as close as they possibly could to the presidential motorcade.[102] As each hour passed and the time of Roosevelt's arrival drew nearer, the party continued full steam ahead. The WPA Leisure Time Band, which was sponsored and organized through the Works Progress Administration, performed a concert of popular music, which blasted through the public address system, yet another reminder of the many ways in which Roosevelt's New Deal programs came to benefit people over the years. Horns tooted, whistles blew, and flags colored the streets red, white and blue. The people did not yet know that the president's arrival would be delayed. So to be safe, two official cars carrying the city mayor and other democratic dignitaries left to greet Roosevelt near the bridge around 4:00 p.m., proving to be there way too early. When news came out of Philadelphia that the motorcade was on its way, the crowd's enthusiasm increased, and they began throwing streamers and confetti into the street that would soon welcome their nation's leader.

The car crossed the bridge closer to 5:00 p.m., and Roosevelt could not miss Camden's enthusiasm. Everywhere he looked, reproductions of his features looked out at him from countless windows, with others draped in American colors. With his car making its way to the plaza, the Democratic Club of Camden took the reigns—literately and figuratively—in leading the procession through the city. Representatives of the civic group drove a donkey attached to an old wagon decorated with pictures of Roosevelt and numerous slogans and excerpts from his past speeches. The back of the cart prominently displayed caricatures of Roosevelt's political opponent, Governor Landon.

"Mr. Mayor and my Camden friends, I am very grateful to you and your city government for this honor, this naming of this plaza for me," began Roosevelt. After initially stopping his speech due to loud applause, the president continued with a twelve-minute talk highlighting the New Deal accomplishments in the state and the nation. His speech was directed to the masses of working-class individuals who looked up to him on the makeshift podium. "Camden is a good cross-section of many different types of people who earn their living—commuters, white-collar workers, factory workers and shipyard workers." He spoke of the bad times and the hope that his New Deal programs had brought to the nation, and he said he hoped they would continue to do so for the next four years. "Today, things are very different," he continued. "None of [these changes] are by chance. They came because your government refused to leave it to chance…. Your government acted!"[103] The crowd erupted in cheers. To the American president, there was no doubt—if ever there was any—of New Jersey's allegiance. Standing behind the rope in the first row was a seventy-five-year-old Mrs. Mary Walters, who rode alone in a bus for hours to see the man for whom she would vote in a week. She arrived at Roosevelt Plaza at 7:30 a.m. and would not leave until after the president spoke. Numerous times, she was approached by police, who offered their assistance, a seat in the press stand or some warm coffee. But she just stood there, persevering. After all, it was not every day that Franklin Delano Roosevelt, arguably the most popular president since Abraham Lincoln, came to town. He finished his speech, the crowd erupted and she finally saw him notice her and wave his hand. She waved back. A week later, President Roosevelt would carry 60 percent of New Jersey's votes and the majority of votes in forty-five other states in the most prominent political landslide in American history up to that point.

IN MANY RESPECTS, FRANKLIN Roosevelt's visits to New Jersey were validations of his New Deal programs, proof that the experiment of 1932 was not a fluke. Still, they were not without controversy. Historians attribute the president's win in 1936 to the so-called New Deal Coalition, or the alignment of various diverse groups, such as women, southern white people, Black Americans, and union workers, supporting the Democratic leader. Yet they also point to the strength of powerful city political organizations, such as the one headed by in Jersey City by Frank Hague, in which services and jobs were often provided for votes. In his second go around, Roosevelt would win the support of America's twelve largest cities.

Roosevelt's reelection came to define the Garden State for years to come. As popular as the president was with the American people following his reelection, the United States was plunged into another recession just a year after Roosevelt visited New Jersey. Forced to cut spending, Roosevelt witnessed the nation's industrial production dropping to pre–New Deal levels. The number of unemployed increased from 7.7 million in 1937 to 10.4 million in 1938.[104] To the many New Jerseyans, the New Deal and, thus, the president had failed them. In the end, it would not be Roosevelt whom many pointed to as the great savior who dragged the Garden State from the depths of the Great Depression. By 1939, it was Europe's war against the fascist threat posed by Germany's Adolf Hitler and Italy's Benito Mussolini that had New Jersey's factories humming to fill orders for the beleaguered nations of Britain and France. The Garden State would finish the decade as a genuine "arsenal of democracy," with its industries, by 1939, employing 433,000 men and women, the highest total since World War I.[105]

The president's visits to New Jersey in October 1936 saw him at the height of his popularity in the Garden State. His victory margin of nearly 20 percent in that election would shrink to 3 percent in 1940 and even further down to 1 percent in 1944. Yet it was the gains that he had made for the Democratic Party in the state in 1936, as seen through Frank Hague's massive exhibitions of support in Jersey City, Bayonne, and Camden, that would transform the traditionally Republican state into a divided swing state for decades to come.

6

NEW JERSEY LIKES IKE

Unlike the other individuals who grace these pages, General Dwight D. Eisenhower was not yet an American president when he visited New Jersey in October 1952. Yet, for all intents and purposes, he might as well have been. Following World War II, General Eisenhower was the most popular man in the United States. In fact, although he was not a politician, the man who was widely viewed as the one person who brought about an end to the hostilities in Europe was sought out to become president by both the Democratic and Republican Parties. His ascendence to the highest office in the nation was a mere formality. All he had to do was declare that he was interested. After rejecting advances by then-president Harry S. Truman to run on a Democratic ticket, Eisenhower became the official Republican nominee on July 11, 1952, during the Republican National Convention in Chicago. With television becoming a new and powerful medium, the American people fell in love with Dwight D. Eisenhower, seeing his big smile in reruns of commercials and fun jingles. "I like Ike" became a slogan of the day, and even Adlai Stevenson, the Democratic nominee, knew there was no contest. This would not be about Democrats or Republicans; this would be about the American people courting the most respected man to lead the nation, not the other way around. New Jersey, a critical swing state, followed the trend. Thus, when Ike announced a two-day tour of the state in October 1952, New Jersey got busy organizing what a local paper called "the most extensive welcome ever given a candidate."[106]

In order to understand the presidential welcome and the hype that Eisenhower's visit elicited in the Garden State, one must first understand the national mood surrounding his acceptance of the nomination for the presidency and the public's fascination with the man himself. While he was unsuccessfully courted by both parties to accept the presidential nomination back in 1948, in January 1952, Ike, a nickname that had stuck with him since childhood, officially declared himself to be a Republican. When he allowed his name to be entered in the party primaries, the "fabulous fifties," as the decade came to be known, was still only a dream.

The future of the Democratic Party under the guidance of Harry Truman was burdened with many obstacles. In Korea, the United Nations forces, under the command and guidance of mostly American military personnel, were brought to a bloody stalemate by the Chinese and North Korean forces. Senator Joseph McCarthy's communist witch hunts at home had created a feeling of fear and distrust, only given further credence by the corruption scandal in the Justice Department's Tax Division. Many complained about the government's ongoing intervention in the national economy, such as the nationalization of the striking steel industry, an action later found to be unconstitutional. Historian Herbert S. Parmet said it best when discussing Eisenhower's ascendance, which he attributed to the phenomena of what appeared to be the general's simultaneous appeal to many people and his great array of interests. "Their desire to have Eisenhower as president was the clearest solution for the plague of corruption, limited wars, twenty years of Democratic rule, communism and greedy labor unions."[107]

The Democrats nominated the little-known and reluctant Governor Adlai E. Stevenson of Illinois in what, from the onset, seemed to be an unequal contest. Eisenhower's broad appeal as the national hero, credited with ending Nazi aggression and saving the world from Hitler and the Axis powers, had great reach on both sides of the aisle. Also noted was the general's moderate political stance, which he called "dynamic conservatism," meaning he was "conservative when it comes to money and liberal when it comes to human beings."[108] But none of this mattered when barely a few days after his trip to New Jersey in mid-October, the soon-to-be president dropped the bombshell that he would end the war in Korea if elected. The few polls that had Stevenson winning the contest by a small margin then gave Ike a clear victory. "For all practical purposes," wrote one reporter, "the contest ended that night."[109]

The enthusiasm that followed the man that would become president of the United States was a creation of advertising experts and machinery, which

A political poster for Dwight D. Eisenhower's 1952 campaign. *Library of Congress.*

orchestrated his rise in popularity in November 1952 before the poll numbers were even in. The campaign managers merchandised Ike the man—his honesty, frankness, and integrity.[110] This would be a victory based almost entirely on the popularity and exploitation thereof of one man whom many identified as the proper successor to former American generals turned presidents, such as Washington, Jackson, and Grant. The campaign strategists inflated and drummed up personal appearances with overreliance on television, radio and advertising campaigns, which brought about the now-famous slogan, "I like Ike." Even if someone was not too sure about who they would vote for, the liberally distributed bumper stickers on millions of cars around the nation reminded them otherwise. He was the man of the people who took the middle road, accepted the social gains of the Roosevelt years, and challenged the centralized power that came out of them. In one commercial, Eisenhower was asked by a citizen on the street about the high cost of living. The elder statesman replied with much humility, "My wife, Mamie, worries about the same thing, and I tell her it's our job to change that on November 4."[111]

The Ike hype train would see the general travel thirty-three miles and deliver over two hundred speeches, forty of which were televised.[112] One of his stops would bring him to the Garden State on October 16, 1952, in a two-day push to firmly place the swing state's Republican-leaning sixteen electoral votes into the GOP presidential column.

"GENERAL EISENHOWER INVADES INDUSTRIAL New Jersey today in a two-day push aimed at placing the Republican-dominated state's sixteen electoral votes in the GOP presidential column!"[113] Although his visit would not last longer than three hours, and even though he was not yet the president of the United States, Ike's visit equaled and even surpassed those of past commanders in chief. Of note was the fact that Eisenhower's visit marked the first time since the Great Depression of the 1930s, apart from a brief

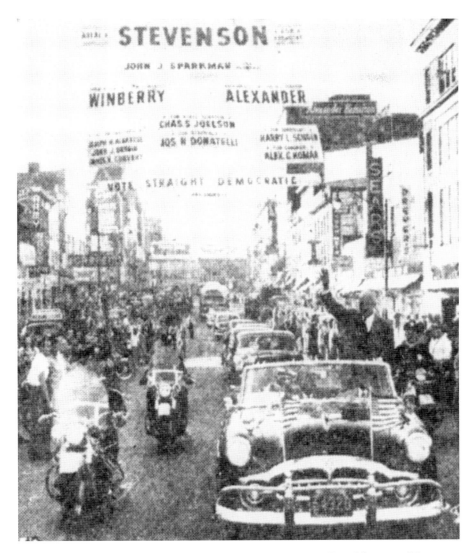

A Democratic banner strung in the business section of Paterson. Republican candidate, Dwight D. Eisenhower, waves from his car as his motorcade passes underneath. Daily Home News *(New Brunswick, NJ), October 17, 1952.*

stint by Wendell Willkie in 1940, that a Republican candidate visited the Garden State. Eisenhower was scheduled to enter the state at noon on Thursday, October 16, 1952, with speeches first in Hackensack and then at the Paterson Armory. The next day was a bit more daunting, calling for a statewide, ten-hour, 150-mile hike through the state, with stops at Camden,

Burlington, Trenton, New Brunswick, Elizabeth, Newark and Jersey City. There was no denying that New Jersey, with its relatively new designation as a swing state, mattered in the 1952 election.

Ike motored into the Garden State from New York City, across the George Washington Bridge, at approximately 12:30 p.m. He was welcomed with a homemade placard held by two admirers. "Don't Worry, Ike, New Jersey is safe," it proclaimed.[114] The sign was not all far from the truth, with the Associated Press releasing the results of a recent study that pointed to Ike's significant New Jersey lead against Stevenson. As he made his way toward Hackensack for a 1:00 p.m. speech and then to Paterson one hour later, Ike's motorcade did not move over twenty miles per hour and reportedly slowed down to ten miles per hour in places where the crowds had gathered to see the soon-to-be president. As if they were preparing for a visit from a head of state, Bergen and Passaic Counties gave all municipal and public employees a half-day holiday. The crowd was further swelled by schoolchildren, who were also given a half-day at all public schools. Equally visible past the massive crowds were countless American flags and strings of triangular flags and fabric in red, white, and blue.

At Ike's first stop in Hackensack, roughly ten thousand official observers looked on as Eisenhower gave his initial GOP speech, accusing the Democrats of giving the American people a double squeeze between high prices and high taxes. One local paper reported homemakers darting from their homes, carrying babies, with toddlers trailing behind, while others leaned from windows of apartment houses and tenements. "Stenographers waved, merchants left their shops and workmen halted factory jobs and gazed through fences."[115] When the motorcade moved from Hackensack toward Paterson, the streets seemed to erupt with thousands of excited voices shouting at the motorcade. The procession was often forced to stop as well-wishers surrounded the open-top vehicle from which a grinning Ike shook hands with all those who managed to get through the police escort on foot and motorcycles. Schoolchildren reportedly darted in and out of the motorcade vehicles, waving small American flags, all while narrowly escaping injury.

Close to one hundred thousand people greeted the general on his four-hour trip to Bergen and Passaic County, the largest turnout for a nonincumbent presidential candidate the state had ever seen. In Paterson, where Ike gave a major political campaign speech, which was carried locally by radio, he was welcomed by the state governor Alfred E. Driscoll and then preceded by a two-hour program. The biggest attraction, apart from the general, that is, was a popular vocal group, the Three Jills and a Jeep. As Ike rode into town under massive banners, one was hard-pressed to miss the Eastside High School, Central High School, Clifton High School, and Passaic High School bands playing at their respective designations throughout the city. Paterson newspapers estimated that approximately forty thousand students were in the crowd, taking advantage of being given time off school to see the national hero speak in their counties. And just in case the crowds got out of hand, Paterson's mayor had ordered all police and fire departments to be fully staffed and at the ready.

As Ike was getting ready to speak at the armory, Governor Driscoll introduced him, finishing his speech with, "In New Jersey, we like Ike," adding, "and we will win with him."[116] The enthusiastic crowd erupted with "We Like Ike!" as the general ascended the stage, unable to stop smiling from ear to ear. Once the group settled, he welcomed the excitement with, "Well, [New Jersey], I like you, too!" And the crowd went wild again. After giving his speech, in which he once again blamed the Democrats for wasteful government spending, Ike promised to fix the national economy and help secure world peace by blocking the expansion of the ever-growing communist threat. The speech ended, and the motorcade turned back for New York so the general could get his much-needed rest before the statewide tour of New Jersey that was scheduled for the next day. Ike made one more stop on his way back. This stop was made in Fair Lawn, where a large crowd watched him receive a key to the White House and a scroll signed by thousands of the town's citizens. To those New Jerseyans who came out to see him on October 16, 1952, this was nothing short of welcoming a national hero who would be their American president in a few short weeks. Looking at the scenes in Bergan and Passaic Counties, there was not much to suggest otherwise come November.

The statewide motorcade through New Jersey began in Camden on the morning of Friday, October 17. That evening, it ended in Jersey City, covering over 150 miles and eight different stops, leaving Eisenhower exhausted yet nearly positive of a Garden State win in the upcoming election. In Camden, a local high school freshman found herself near the departing Eisenhower as the police were moving people aside for the general to get into his car. She politely asked for his autograph. While Ike declined and said he was running late, he told her to write to him at the Commodore Hotel in New York and said that he would be happy to send her one. She received the autograph within a few days with a short note thanking her for her support. After a somewhat exuberant welcome in Trenton, where the Mercer County

Ike Tells Voters to Demand Government They Can Respect

8,000 Turn Out For Rally

By FRANK M. DEINER

"You decide between now and November 4th what you want to do, but above all, try to get the government you know and respect because that will be for the good of America and that will mean your good." General Dwight D. Eisenhower, Republican presidential candidate admonished a crowd of 8,000 who greeted him yesterday at Court House Square in his tour of New Jersey.

The Republican presidential candidate was cheered when he stepped to the podium and he was cheered when he was introduced by U. S. Senator H. Alexander Smith who substituted for Governor Alfred E. Driscoll. The Governor left the motorcade at Trenton and went to Newark for a night meeting.

Turn to page three for full page of pictures of General Eisenhower's visit to this city.

General Eisenhower arrived at the court house about 4:35 p.m. as the huge crowd was growing restive. He had been scheduled to speak at 4 p. m. but long before that hour the crowd had begun to assemble. Some Republicans were in the square at 1 p. m. At 4 p. m. there was a compact crowd in front of the court house which spilled into Bayard street.

The crowd extended into Elm Row with many taking up places in the windows of the county buildings and City Hall. The steps of the New Brunswick Savings Institution, City Hall, and the postoffice opposite the court house were jammed with people, while a large crowd gathered outside the Paterson street entrance of the court house.

They began to chant "We Want Ike," when the smiling general with arms uplifted moved through the main court room to the rostrum for his introduction. There was a mighty roar as the crowd caught a glimpse of him.

It was the general's second visit to New Jersey in his campaign to nail down the state's 16 electoral votes. He had toured Bergen and Passaic counties on Thursday when he was greeted by crowds estimated up to 100,000.

Biggest Ever

While the street crowds were larger in other counties nowhere was the rally crowd larger than in New Brunswick. It was the largest political gathering ever witnessed in Middlesex county and presented the Democrats with a real challenge to surpass when President Harry S. Truman comes here Tuesday.

It was an enthusiastic crowd notwithstanding that General

An attentive crowd stretching to the rooftop of the Lawyers Building at Bayard street and Elm row listens as General Eisenhower speaks from the steps of the County Court House. Close-up of G.O.P. standard bearer is at left.

General Was Late, But Crowd Stayed to Cheer Him Lustily

Republicans Make Most of Their Big Day for Ike; Party's Top Brass Very Much in Evidence

By ELIHU JOSEPH

"Give 'Em Hell, Ike" and "Pour it On, Ike," said the signs, but early hour the general, speaking extemporaneously, preferred to dwell upon the American Heritage and touched only lightly on "the mess in hand shortly after lunch to arrange last-minute details for the Washington." The fervor of the crowd that visit of their party leader.

speakers' platform had been erected, began gathering at an largest political gathering ever Mr. Lederman, county G.O.P. chairman, Dr. Nathanael Frankel and other party leaders were on

Republicans staged a large rally for Ike at the War Memorial Building, he headed for perhaps the largest event of the day in New Brunswick. Apart from the large street crowds that were reminiscent of the crowds from the previous day, Ike's appearance in the capital of Middlesex County at New Brunswick's Court House Square "was the largest political gathering ever witnessed in [that part of the state]."[117] By the time he arrived, the crowd had swelled to nearly ten thousand strong, packing in shoulder to shoulder in a square that was not meant to hold their number.

Arriving thirty minutes late, the smiling general lifted his arms as he approached the six-by-six-foot podium that had been set up for him at

Opposite: A newspaper clip showing General Eisenhower speaking from the steps of the county courthouse in New Brunswick as an attentive crowd listens on. Daily Home News *(New Brunswick, NJ), October 18, 1952.*

Left: Presidential candidate Dwight Eisenhower and his wife, Mamie Eisenhower, seated at a campaign event. *Library of Congress.*

the steps of the county courthouse. As he made his way through the main courtroom, Ike heard the loud chants outside: "We Want Ike!" The roar from the crowd was deafening as Ike finally emerged. He looked down at the thousands of Republican supporters and pointed to some homemade signs with thumbs up in acknowledgment. Some of the more prominent signs read, "Give 'Em Hell, Ike," and "Pour It On, Ike."[118] Not seen were the signs held by some Rutgers and New Jersey College students in the back of the crowd who favored Ike's opponent, Stevenson. When the county campaign chairman handed Eisenhower a large broom "to sweep out the mess in the national capital," the crowd erupted by signing "Happy Birthday." The police and the national guard reserves strained to keep the crowd back from the presidential nominee and the nearly two hundred special guests and Republican dignitaries set up before him on the steps of the courthouse.

The general began his address by thanking New Jerseyans for the amazing reception: "One of the things that I have learned is that New Jersey seems to take its politics seriously, with a lot of enthusiasm, and I've seen a lot of it yesterday and today," chuckled Eisenhower.[119] After acknowledging that as an American citizen, he was free to criticize the party in power—a blatant dig directed at the communist Soviet Union—he instead chose to concentrate not on smearing his opponent but on outlining a better tomorrow for average Americans. He brought his address to a close with a plea to his voters: "You decide between now and November 4 what you want to do, but above all, try to get the government you know and respect because that will be for the good of America, and that will mean your good."[120] After much cheering and other chants of "I Like Ike," the general stepped down and made his way to his car for a trip to nearby Elizabeth and Newark. In a comical turn of events, just as Ike was about to get into his car, a middle-aged woman freed herself from the police barricade and ran toward the general, embracing him in what some newspapers described as "a half nelson." As a result, the general took a few extra minutes to speak to some well-wishers before getting into his automobile and departing for his next stop.

Police estimates indicated that seventy-five thousand people saw the general in Camden, Trenton, New Brunswick, Elizabeth, Newark and Jersey City. Already worn down after a full day of appearances, the future president freshened himself up when he arrived in Newark by taking a shower and changing from a brown suit to a navy blue one. It was in Newark that Ike delivered a major address on civil rights when he spoke to a crowd of thousands assembled in the Mosque Theatre. Picking northern New Jersey as the place to highlight his agenda due to its large Black population, the Republican candidate pledged himself to a nationwide fight for human rights that he would personally lead if elected. "If I am elected, I will confer with the governors of the forty-eight states and urge them to take the lead in their states in guaranteeing the economic rights of all our citizens." He finished the speech by condemning poll taxes and the McCarran Act, which regulated immigration. Uncharacteristic in relation to all other New Jersey speeches, Ike did go on the offensive against Truman, who had been slandering him in the press, giving the American people false hope by reminding his Newark audience that it was President Truman who once voted against lifting poll taxes.

Ike would conclude his tour of the Garden State with perhaps the largest fervor yet seen in Jersey City. The reception was the most ironic and significant sign of political paradigm shifts in the Garden State, as Jersey City had been the heart of the state's Democratic Party not long before. The newspapers did not mince words: "25,000 Cheer Ike in Hague's Town," screamed the headline of the *Wilmington Morning News*. Port Huron, Michigan's *Times Herald*, was blunt: "25,000 persons greeted [Ike] Friday night in Jersey City—a Democratic stronghold once ruled by 'boss' Frank Hague," adding, "Hague clearly no longer controls the Democratic organization there."[121] The corrupt mayor had retired five years prior, after the appointment of Republican governor Alfred Driscoll. The latter curbed corruption with actions like installing voting machines throughout the state. With crowds

President Eisenhower waving from his presidential limousine as it makes its way through Hackensack. *Joseph Bilby.*

nearing thirty thousand converged into Journal Square, the Republican candidate did not disappoint, praising the state and acknowledging the support he was receiving in "the hometown of Frank Hague." He was clearly pale and looked exhausted as he mounted the platform for his final appearance in the Garden State. After delivering a speech similar in context to those he had delivered earlier, he bid his supporters farewell and left behind what the *Hackensack Record* called "one of the biggest crowds ever to assembled in Journal Square for a presidential or another political candidate."[122] Exhausted, Ike retired back to New York that evening. It was the last time he would visit the state as a mere candidate. The next time

Eisenhower spent any considerable time in the Garden State, it would be as the president of the United States. And he would visit in a less formal capacity, simply playing a round of golf.

LOST WITHIN THE "I Like Ike" crusade through New Jersey in October 1952—and perhaps significant in its own right—was the state tour by the actual president of the United States, Harry S. Truman, which followed on the heels of the famous general. It proved to be a bitter campaign by an outgoing president in favor of the Democratic nominee Adlai Stevenson, which, if anything, highlighted the shifting allegiances of New Jerseyans to the Republican Party. This was also not the first time that President Truman visited the Garden State, having done so on a quick swing through the state's Democratic strongholds on his way to a surprising victory in the 1948 election. The event was forever symbolized by the image of a grinning Truman holding up the misprinted *Chicago Daily Tribune*, which prematurely announced his opponent, New York governor Thomas E. Dewey's, win. Ironically, his stop in New Jersey that year, as grand as it was, turned out to be not quite enough, as he would lose the Garden State to the Republican governor. In what the press would refer to as Jersey City boss Frank Hague's "sort of election eve confessional" for president, the mayor welcomed Truman for a tour of the state, even after going on the record to state that "Harry Truman would lose New Jersey by 300,000."[123]

The New Jersey Democratic State Headquarters announced President Harry S. Truman's one-hundred-mile-long whistle-stop tour of the Garden State one day after Ike started his. Not wasting much time, the president began his tour mere days after the general on October 21, 1952. Beginning in Jersey City, the motorcade would include stops and addresses by the president in Jersey City, Newark, Elizabeth, New Brunswick, Trenton and Camden. Unlike 1948, this time around, Truman was not courting New Jerseyans to follow him but instead urged them to stick with his Democratic Party by casting their vote for Adlai E. Stevenson. Truman and his party might have been down and out, with all indicators suggesting that there would be no repeat of the 1948 upset, but he was still the president of the United States, and he was coming to town.

If this was a game of numbers, the presidential tag attached to Harry Truman still carried more weight than that of a winning World War II general. Still, the trip did not go as smoothly as anticipated, and there was at least some indication that New Jersey "Liked Ike." The police estimates indicated that, in total, about 400,000 people came out to see the president across all his stops in the state. Camden's *Courier Post*, a Democratic-leaning newspaper, proudly proclaimed, "Mr. Truman outdrew Republican presidential candidate Dwight D. Eisenhower, who car-hopped the state last Friday."[124] In fact, the chief executive was greeted in Newark by a police-estimated crowd of 250,000, "the largest political reception in New Jersey history."[125] Other newspapers across the state were a bit more vague with their assessments, simply stating, "Truman Crowds Amazing," or "the President was

President Truman speaking from the steps of Camden City Hall as he made a bid for the city's vote for Adlai Stevenson. Courier Post *(Camden, NJ), October 22, 1952.*

wildly acclaimed almost everywhere."[126] Passaic's *Herald News* was quick to point out that the people were mostly there to see the president of the United States, not to support a specific party, perhaps giving more credence to Eisenhower's visit the week before. In the end, "the big majority of those who thronged the streets to the president were schoolkids and [others] who composed the bulk of Eisenhower's crowds Friday," wrote one reporter on the scene.

Although the weather was much colder than it was when Ike visited the state a week prior, the six-hour tour saw the president riding in a Cadillac convertible with the top down the entire time. As if in a sign of toughness, Truman made sure he took off his coat and hat and left them in the car at each scheduled speaking stop. Following in a car behind him the entire trip was his twenty-eight-year-old aspiring actress daughter, Margaret, who, at every stop, "flashed her famous smile, waved a daintily gloved hand, wrapped her brown poodle coat tighter, and then vanished from the platform."[127] Being very much part of the show, with her father pointing her out as one of his greatest assets, the "first daughter" was handed bouquets by admiring women and children at each stop. While his daughter was garnering much attention in each city, Truman stuck to the script and continued to belittle General Eisenhower and the GOP's campaign. Seemingly every speech ended with the crowds chanting "Give 'em hell, Harry" and "You tell 'em,

Harry." In Newark, where the president spoke in front of city hall, "the air was filled with paper tossed from windows and rooftops," and "twenty-one aerial bombs burst in a presidential salute as a dozen bands struck up 'Hail to the Chief.'"[128]

Still, this was not the candidate, Adlai Stevenson, personally campaigning for president; it was instead an official visit from Harry Truman, the president of the United States. There was no denying the fact that as much of an honor as a presidential visit is to any town, city, or state, New Jersey was ready for Ike to be president, and it greeted him as if he already was. Perhaps foreshadowing the outcome of the November 4 election, when speaking in Trenton, Truman was heckled with chants of "We Like Ike," which he appeared not to notice. When in New Brunswick, the Rutgers students this time decided to repeat their feat of opposing famous visitors. Instead of protesting Eisenhower, as they had done a week prior, they chanted "We like Ike" as Truman's motorcade passed them.[129] The biggest repudiation of the current president came in Trenton, where two eggs sailed past Truman's head as he spoke to nearly five thousand people from the steps of the statehouse; missing him, the projectiles landed in the press section, twenty-five feet from the president. *New York Daily News* photographer Fred Morgan and WMTR Morristown radio station host Merrill Morris, who became the beneficiaries of the flying gifts, would go on to tell their friends that they took one for the president.[130]

The next time President Truman came to visit the Garden State was on September 1, 1961. The then-seventy-seven-year-old former president and his wife went to Paramus to watch their singer-actress daughter star in Bergen Mall Playhouse's opening performance of *The Time of the Cuckoo*. By then, the local papers relegated Truman's visit to the interior pages. Yet it seemed like the rift that was on full display years earlier in the Garden State between Truman and Ike was not yet settled. When asked by a local newspaperman before the show about the recently elected president John F. Kennedy, Truman said, "He has guts enough to make a decision, something his predecessor never had."[131]

WHILE 1952 SHOULD HAVE been the year of the presidential visit of Harry S. Truman, it was eclipsed, just as it had been at the time, by the bigger story of the visit of the soon-to-be president Dwight D. Eisenhower. And while Ike would not stump in New Jersey during his reelection campaign in 1956, we can now say that two American presidents came to the Garden State in October 1952, one of them just did not know it yet—or perhaps he did. Speaking after Ike's stump through New Jersey, the state's governor Alfred E. Driscoll concluded, "Eisenhower touched the hearts and minds of Jersey men and women yesterday," adding, "On the basis of the turnouts in the former Democratic strongholds of Camden, Trenton, New Brunswick, Elizabeth, Newark, and Jersey City, I believe New Jersey will go for General Eisenhower by at least a 185,000 majority in the November election."[132] When it was all said and done, Dwight D. Eisenhower would carry New Jersey by a margin of 14.83 percent, winning eighteen out of the state's twenty-one counties. This was indeed a big change considering that Franklin D. Roosevelt had won the Garden State in all of his four national victories in the 1930s and 1940s. On November 4, 1952, Eisenhower won the nation in what amounted to a landslide, finally justifying New Jersey's presidential-level welcome he received when he toured the Garden State the month before.

JOHNSONMANIA ECLIPSES KENNEDY

When examining the glamour of President John F. Kennedy's Camelot years, with all his wealth, education, fame and a beautiful wife by his side, one may get lost in the thought that the extent of his popularity had no bounds. Yet on the eve of the 1960 election, the junior senator from Massachusetts, epitomized by his charm and youth in life and tragedy in death, had far from captured the hearts of all his fellow citizens. During his late October visit to New Jersey, the national Kennedy-mania was still stuck in second gear. He was not yet president when he visited New Jersey, and unlike Ike, only a few believed that he would win the coveted position. His opponents often criticized the man for being more image than substance. Lyndon B. Johnson in 1964, not Kennedy in 1960, would be the great savior that the Garden State Democrats hoped for in overturning the Eisenhower gains in the state. And although Kennedy never visited New Jersey as the president of the United States, his somewhat lackluster showing in 1960 paled in comparison to that of Johnson four years later. Lyndon B. Johnson, with his Texas drawl, middle-class upbringing, plain Jane wife, and brutish looks and demeanor, left a much greater mark on New Jersey during his October 1964 visit than the glamorous Kennedy ever could.

Historians do not shy away from researching and writing about the 1960 battle for America's highest office. In one corner was the young and exuberant senator from Massachusetts riding the high of the Kennedy name and money (his father, Joseph P. Kennedy, was the onetime U.S. ambassador to Germany and a major stock market and commodity investor). Opposing the young Jack Kennedy, as he was known to his friends, was the incumbent vice president of the United States under Dwight D. Eisenhower, Richard Milhous Nixon, a much more serious and imposing figure. Although not entirely sold on the Kennedy glamour, the American people leaned toward Kennedy's energy and, at least in the North, his willingness to take on civil rights issues, something that his opponent did not fully embrace. Historians credit the first-ever televised presidential debate for pulling the young and inexperienced Kennedy past Nixon, a veteran and career politician. Even though Kennedy was less knowledgeable than Nixon, in him, the seventy million people who watched on their TV sets saw a man who was cool, collected, and fit for office. On the other hand, the vice president, still weakened by his recent bout with illness, appeared uncomfortable, perspiring and unshaven. As the story goes, those who heard the debate on the radio believed that Nixon had won, while those at home had no illusions about Kennedy's superiority.

Jack Kennedy arrived in New Jersey on November 7, 1960, less than twenty-four hours before the national election on November 8—it was his last campaign stop before returning home to await the election results the next day. Contrary to the Kennedy myth, it was not as glamorous as the eventual old newsreels of the smiling president would have one believe. The senator's twin-engine private airplane, called *Caroline* after his daughter, had arrived at Teterboro Airport two hours late. There, newspapers reported that many people had given up and simply gone home instead of waiting for the young Kennedy. With a blatant dig at his eventual predecessor, Eisenhower, an avid golfer, Jack took up the amplifier and announced to the two thousand people who had gathered to greet him at the airport, "I am sorry I am late, but I haven't been playing golf. We're working twenty-four hours a day to return this country to a responsible, progressive government!"[133]

After a brief speech at the airport, Kennedy was greeted at the Teaneck Armory by an overflowing crowd of twelve thousand at a venue that was meant to only hold slightly more than half that number. Like in other cities, the crowds roared in welcome as soon as they saw the young senator. The *Paterson Evening News* reported how "the police lines buckled as women surged to touch their party's handsome standard-bearer," adding how "pretty girls in white surrounded the speakers' stand with 'Blackjack' signs."[134] When hoards of news photographers blocked the public's view by standing upon Kennedy's arrival at the armory, the people promptly booed them to sit down. Amused by the scene, Jack expressed to the crowd that getting the

The scene of November 6, 1960, at the Jersey City Democratic Rally, where presidential candidate John F. Kennedy spoke as he wound up his final tour of New Jersey. Vineland *(NJ)* Times Journal, *November 7, 1960.*

reporters to listen only made him more confident that the New Jerseyans' commanding nature would make him victorious.

From Teterboro, Kennedy arrived at the Mosque Auditorium in Essex County, the state's largest and most pivotal county. With ten thousand people reportedly waiting outside to see him enter and exit, the four thousand labor leaders who were invited inside listened, albeit only politely, to his speech sponsored by the state's American Federation of Labor Committee. Just minutes after Kennedy's departure, the labor leaders reportedly took off their Kennedy pins, took out their "Case for Senator" buttons, and went

Senator John F. Kennedy using an amplifier to address the crowd at New Jersey's Teterboro Airport on the eve of the 1960 election. With him is New Jersey governor Robert B. Meyner. Vineland *(NJ)* Times Journal, *November 7, 1960.*

upstairs in the adjacent Essex House Hotel to attend a labor reception for Senator Clifford P. Chase, the Republican candidate for reelection.[135] Meanwhile, outside, the crowds blocked the motorcade and refused to move until Jack stood on top of a flatbed truck and briefly addressed them. "Did you touch him?" a little girl asked one reporter. "Did you ever shake hands with him?" a little boy asked another.[136] Kennedy waved at the crowd and then briskly disappeared into his limousine, which was already late for his speech at the largest rally of the night in Jersey City, the state's Democratic center.

A fairly standard affair, the Jersey City rally was nonetheless a bit underwhelming with its crowd, which had supposedly peaked at sixty thousand, yet diminished by the time of Kennedy's late arrival, as "many had gone home when the hour became late."[137] This was still a massive improvement from his brief visit to the city in September 1960, when he spoke to a crowd of roughly five thousand people after first speaking to a similar number at the Bergen Mall. This time around, the Kennedy hype train was at its peak, and even then, it somehow seemed to be less enthusiastic than it should have been, especially when compared with the visit to the state by Lyndon B. Johnson four years later.

After thanking the crowd for making his last speech outside of New England a memorable one, Kennedy and his entourage motored to Newark Airport toward his private plane, which was brought over from Teterboro. The next day, Kennedy managed to win only seven out of twenty-one New Jersey counties. He snuck out of New Jersey with 49.96 percent of the vote to Nixon's 49.16 percent, a barely visible margin of 0.80 percent. It was not the refutation of the eight years under Republican rule that the New Jersey Democrats had hoped for. Yet, unlike how the popular history narrative might want to make us believe, it would not be Kennedy but Johnson, albeit until the escalation of the Vietnam War, who would return the Democratic Party to its New Deal glory.

"IT WASN'T BEATLEMANIA AT [Bergen] Mall; It was Johnsonmania!" bellowed the headline of the *Paterson News* on October 15, 1964. President Johnson's visit to the Garden State on the eve of the 1964 election was the epitome of a celebrity frenzy, and Johnson was the epitome of a celebrity president. Who would have thought that the brash man from Texas, whose six-foot-four-inch figure towered over all those around him and whose infamous "Johnson treatment" of clinching people's hands and intimidating them by invading their personal space while talking, was a campaign darling? Yet that is exactly what he was, which was on full display in Bergen County in 1964.

The dichotomy of Lyndon Baines Johnson's presidency could perhaps only be rivaled by that of the slave-owning and slave-condemning Thomas Jefferson. Johnson was on his way to becoming one of the greatest American presidents of all time. The Democratic Party initially hailed him as the next Roosevelt—yet all of that changed when the Vietnam War demonstrated his failure in leading the nation. The conflict compromised any credibility Johnson had built up through his domestic programs, forever tarnishing his legacy. By the time antiwar protesters paraded in front of the White House, infamously chanting, "LBJ, how many kids did you kill today?" Johnson's critical domestic achievements were all forgotten. This was quite significant,

Delegates on the floor at the 1964 Democratic National Convention in Atlantic City, New Jersey. They are holding a large banner for Lyndon B. Johnson. *Library of Congress.*

as Johnson was instrumental in passing Medicare and Medicaid, signing the comprehensive Civil Rights Act of 1964, and the Voting Rights Act of 1965. By 1968, New Jerseyans had canceled the media darling whom they once welcomed with open arms and festivities compared to visits from rock 'n' roll superstars. Johnson was a failed leader who lost his great aspirations in the jungles of Vietnam. But none of that was relevant on Wednesday, October 15, 1964, at New Jersey's Bergen Mall.

In order to understand the media frenzy that surrounded Johnson and the overexuberant reaction to his visit, one needs to understand what his wife, Lady Bird Johnson, alluded to in an early interview: "Some men are born to campaign, and Lyndon was."[138] Following the assassination of John F. Kennedy, Johnson threw himself into campaigning for the first time as the incumbent leader of the Democratic Party. His opponent, the ultraconservative Arizona senator Barry Goldwater brought the far right to center stage, something that most of the country, apart from the Deep South, was not yet ready to embrace. Thus, it seemed that the stump was not about winning against Goldwater but about breaking Democratic records and attaining the landslide that the ambitious Johnson so badly desired. For forty-two days before November 4, 1964, the American president peregrinated the country, traveling over sixty thousand miles and making nearly two hundred speeches, "promising peace and prosperity and warning against the threat to both by his opponent."[139] And through it, he loved every second. Even before he arrived in the Garden State, the people knew what to expect from their commander in chief. Johnson interacted with his crowds more like a rock star than a serious politician. He would often leave his motorcade and walk up to the crowds of people to shake their hands. His hand was swollen and even bleeding after hours of "pressing flesh," and his aides had to bandage them frequently.[140]

Even before Johnson's plane had touched down in Teterboro, the people of New Jersey knew that this was not going to be a barricaded, no-touch type of visit, where they might catch a glimpse of the president as he waves from the back of his limousine. So, getting to the predetermined staging areas ahead of time was key, especially for the young people who saw this as a chance to meet their favorite celebrity. He may not have been Elvis Presley, but Johnson was still the president of the United States and one who was not afraid to mingle with the crowd. Dubbed by the press "Mr. Average Everyday American," the thirty-sixth president kicked off his campaign on April 11, when he walked over to the southeast gate of the White House, disregarding the pleas of his secret servicemen. He called over to the people who were

Left: President Lyndon B. Johnson greets well-wishers at the Bergen Mall visit in 1964. A Band-Aid is visible on his right hand, covering a wound associated with his predisposition to shake everyone's hand. Morning Call *(Paterson, NJ), October 15, 1964.*

Right: President Johnson prepares to leave the Teterboro Airport. He shook more hands before the secret service whisked him away to the awaiting plane. Morning Call *(Paterson, NJ), October 15, 1964.*

walking by on the other side. After ordering that the gate be opened to let about one hundred individuals in, Johnson yelled, "All right, all you ugly men go up there [in the back] and all you pretty girls stay here with me." He then proceeded to give them all a private tour of the White House while dispelling stories of his childhood and ascendance to the highest office in the nation.[141] He continued these improv meetings and walks from time to time, always to the surprise of those lucky individuals who happened to be passing the White House on that given day.

Instead of the comforts of Democratic Essex or Hudson Counties, Lyndon B. Johnson chose to hold his rally in the state's Republican stronghold of Bergen County. After Johnson stepped out of the presidential DC-6 airplane, it took mere moments for him to become the affable politician New Jerseyans saw on television. Impatient throughout the New Jersey governor Richard J. Hughes's welcoming speeches and greetings from U.S. state senators, Johnson hastily made his way toward the low fence at Teterboro Airport to shake hands with his supporters. The president, wearing a gray fedora and a tan raincoat, paid no attention to the pandemonium that broke out around him as "a waggling tangle of arms and grasping hands" reached for him.[142] The 130 uniformed police officers brought in to keep order desperately tried to keep Johnson from being crushed. Unfazed, the president continued flashing his signature grin as the Pascack Valley High School Band played "Hello Lyndon" to the beat of a Broadway musical hit tune. It truly was a scene of mayhem, with the overwhelmed and visibly unhappy secret service agents attempting to steer the commander in chief to his motorcade.

In the end, not unlike the Beatles or Elvis, Lyndon Baines Johnson was swept toward his limousine as the three-thousand-strong crowd, with a plethora of reporters, photographers, fans, both young and old, began jumping the safety lines behind him. As the hoard moved closer to the waiting motorcade, an undismayed Johnson "touched hands with shrieking teenagers and near-hysterical bystanders."[143] This was all very much distressing, if not downright shocking to the secret service, as it had been less than a year since the fatal shooting of President John F. Kennedy. To those in charge of his protection, Johnson was acting irresponsibly, and as much as the local population loved his New Jersey visit, it was a sheer nightmare for his bodyguards. The Garden State also did not take the visit lightly, especially with images from Dallas and Dealey Plaza the previous November still entrenched in people's minds. Uniformed police officers guarded every overpass and intersection on the route from the airport to the Bergen Mall in Paramus. Routes 46, 17, and 4 resembled Fort Knox, with police cars, blue-uniformed men and women, and even national guardsmen visible in every direction. A state police captain also added that he had an undisclosed number of plain-clothes detectives around the president at all times.

To keep security tight, no crowds were allowed to congregate on the presidential route except at predetermined sites, where small groups of spectators assembled to watch the motorcade pass residential areas off Routes 46, 17, and 4.[144] The many people who waited along the motorcade's route knew that the extra security was warranted; all they had to do was pay attention to the presidential Lincoln car. Newspapers were very blunt: "President Rides in Death Car," proclaimed the *Paterson News*. Many recognized the renovated touring car in which President Kennedy was assassinated in Dallas as it passed by them on New Jersey roads. The 1961 Lincoln Continental, today displayed at the Henry Ford Museum, was driven from Washington to the Garden State with other secret service vehicles. It was a grim reminder that the people of New Jersey should not take such an open visit by an American president for granted—not after 1963.

The crowd, between twenty-five thousand and thirty thousand strong, arrived at the Bergen Mall around 8:00 a.m., even though the president was not expected for another two hours. By 9:00 a.m., the people were packed shoulder to shoulder, waiting for the arrival of the commander in chief. Although many notable stars of the time were listed on the entertainment program, such as Barbara Streisand, Tony Bennett and Lauren Bacall, not many actually showed up to cheer on the crowds. The stage was commandeered by Morey Amsterdam, a well-known comedian and supporting actor on the *Dick Van Dyke Show*, who acted as the master of the ceremonies. As thousands of the president's impatient fans waited for a sign of his arrival, the stage near the Bergan Mall had become a revolving act of various famous celebrities. While it may seem perfectly normal in modern times for politicians to court favorite popular culture artists to speak on their behalf and entertain their supporters at rallies, this was still a relatively new practice in 1964. By 10:00 a.m., when circling military helicopters gave the indication that Johnson's arrival was imminent, the masses had heard speeches from the likes of Anthony Perkins from the 1960 movie *Psycho* and fellow actors Roddy McDowell, Shelly Winters and the Oscar-winning Jan Sterling.

Paramus's continued security precautions were seen on Johnson's route toward the mall as police officers walked along the mall's rooftops, carrying rifles and walkie-talkies. Below them was pandemonium, perhaps the largest of any of the presidential visits to New Jersey before or since. A section was set up for the press to the right of the president's platform, and all the reporters had to go through background checks to receive a special pass to be this close to Johnson. Ironically, the security measure seemed futile, as teenagers and adults who were eager to see the president crowded into the restricted area and jumped on tables to secure a better view. The overwhelmed police officers watched helplessly as some of the tables within the section collapsed, bringing down the teenagers with them. "Take one step back!" pleaded police officers who were assigned to

President Lyndon B. Johnson reaches his hand out to greet a crowd of supporters at Bergen Mall. *Library of Congress.*

the section. At one point, an eleven-year-old girl was rendered unconscious and had to be revived in an area behind the police barricade. Another woman was placed on a stretcher and carried to a nearby ambulance. Five other women had to be put into a police car to recuperate from dizziness and injuries incurred from the crowding.[145]

President Johnson arrived at 10:12 a.m. His covered limousine, proceeded by police cars, two secret service cars, and four secret service men running alongside the president's car, made its way through the double ropes that were put up on the roadway from Route 4 up to the platform. On each side were crowds of people from various Bergen communities with large signs. One proclaimed, "Ridgewood Backs Lyndon." The limousine was stopped by some one thousand young women and girls who were members of the Young Democrats for Johnson; they were ornated in red, white, and blue ribbons and holding massive banners. As Johnson exited the vehicle, news reports admitted, "There was no controlling the crowd," adding that "the ropes fell, and a screaming mob ran toward the platform."[146] Police and secret service agents formed a chain around the commander in chief as he made his way up the high, secured platform. Johnson remained in character, managing to shake hands with those near him. He even exchanged words with some of his fans before the security forced him up the ramp.

The tall Texan, dressed in a black suit, kept the crowd in a "frenzy" as he moved to each corner of the platform, shaking hands and waving. "The president, whose hands have been sore from hand shaking, had a band-aid on one of his hands and merely touched hands with those fortunate to get near to touch him," reported one bystander.[147] When he began speaking, young girls near the stage erupted in screams of excitement as if it was not a fifty-six-year-old gruff politician but some teen heartthrob looking down on them. Johnson delivered only half of his prepared speech on account of a sore throat and persistent hoarseness, which was attributed to his heavy campaign schedule. He drove home his bipartisan message that electing the far-right Goldwater would be akin to "repealing the present and vetoing the future."[148] In line with his "Great Society" domestic policy, which was aimed at bettering the lives of all Americans, regardless of sex, creed, or race, the president added, "The people do not want the White House to be a house where some citizens are privileged to enter, and others are turned away at the door because they were born 'wrong' or because they believe 'wrong' or because they voted 'wrong.'" After that statement, the crowd erupted in one continuous cheer that allowed Johnson to take a moment to clear his throat.

Standing silently amid the cheering crowds were fifteen people holding up seven replicas of coffins, each bearing a different name and date but all with the same message. The New Jersey chapter of the Congress of Racial Equality (CORE) was there as a somber reminder that Johnsonmania was not as great and pure as the crowds around them suggested—a foreshadowing of sorts, perhaps. One of the signs read, "Murdered, No Arrests." Three of the names on the coffins reflected three young civil rights activists—two white, one Black—whose recent disappearance, murder and eventual discovery in a shallow grave in Mississippi had sparked a national manhunt that had captured the minds of the American people. This was 1964, and the race issue was far from resolved. When the motorcade entered and later left the lot of the Bergen Mall, it had no choice but to drive past the CORE group. "He saw us," said one of the members, "he saw us."[149]

When it was all said and done, the president spoke for roughly seven minutes, but the crowd that showed up to see him did not mind. As he was escorted down from the platform for his trip back to the airport, the bubble-

CORE Unit Adds Grim Note To LBJ Bergen Mall Rally

They stood silently amid a | motorcade entered the lot from
cheering throng in the sparkling | Teterboro Airport the cars,

Even among all the 1964 glamour surrounding Lyndon B. Johnson's visit to New Jersey, there were signs that showed not everyone got to participate in his "great society." Herald News *(Passaic, NJ), October 17, 1964.*

top limousine was twice surrounded by people, prompting Johnson to get out to wave, smile, and once again grasp the outstretched arms "with his own scratched and swollen hands."[150] One delighted recipient of Johnson's handshake was a young mother who was holding a young baby. "We just came to see the president," she said, beaming with happiness.[151] "Great show.… One of the best," glared Johnson at Democratic county chairman Daniel Amster as he returned to Teterboro Airport for the flight to more campaigning in Pennsylvania and New York.[152] He was not wrong. Just a few years earlier, when his predecessor, John F. Kennedy, spoke to New Jerseyans at the same Bergen Mall, his crowd comprised five thousand men and women; this time, Johnson knocked it out of the ballpark. Considering the grand spectacle awarded to him—and in the state's Republican epicenter nonetheless—there was not much doubt among even his opponents that President Johnson would be the first Democrat since Franklin D. Roosevelt to win the coveted county and the state.

PRESIDENT LYNDON B. JOHNSON carried New Jersey in a landslide with an astronomical voting margin of 31.75 percent. His reception in Bergen in October was not a fluke, as the Democratic leader managed to sweep all twenty-one of New Jersey's counties—the first and, to this day, the only Democratic presidential nominee to have ever done this. Ironically, it would be the last time until 1992 that the Garden State would vote Democratic in the presidential election. For Johnson and the Democrats, 1964 was a win on all fronts, with forty other northern Democratic congressmen elected to office, giving the president a majority in Congress, the likes of which had not been seen since Roosevelt's 1936 election. Yet this would all be short-lived for Johnson and his party.

Lyndon Baines Johnson would never again be as popular in New Jersey or the nation as he was on that brisk October day at the Bergen Mall. The nation's plunge into the Vietnam War, together with growing domestic frustration with the ongoing war and the slow progress of attaining equal rights for minorities, led to unforeseen consequences at home. The war divided the nation, with critics blaming the president for its escalation by implementing the draft, increasing troops, and bombing North Vietnam. Johnson quickly became the scapegoat. The people blamed him for dragging the United States into a conflict they did not want, and it was becoming harder for the president to deny the charge. In 1963, under Kennedy, the United States had about twenty thousand military personnel in Indochina. In 1967, three years into Johnson's presidency, that number exceeded four hundred thousand. As the antimilitary movement grew across college campuses and tens of thousands of men evaded the draft in a refusal to fight, public opinion polls showed that Johnson had lost much of the popularity he exhibited with voters that day in 1964 in New Jersey.

Meanwhile, domestic violence was spreading across the nation. New Jersey was not immune to the riots that broke out in many inner-city neighborhoods. The Black community of Newark exploded in July 1967, leading to four long days of rioting, burning, and millions of dollars' worth of property loss and damage. Twenty-three people died in the riots, and hundreds more were injured. According to Thomas Fleming, it hastened the exodus of manufacturers and merchants. "The city lost twenty-three thousand private jobs between 1967 and 1972 and was labeled a dying city."[153] And just like what was experienced in Detroit and Los Angeles around the same time, the breakdown of society into violence was attributed to the lack of leadership coming from Washington.

Johnsonmania was over. Recognizing that the Vietnam War and domestic violence had made his reelection impossible, Lyndon B. Johnson withdrew his presidential candidacy in March 1968. More violence would erupt that year, with the assassinations of both Dr. Martin Luther King Jr. and Senator Robert F. Kennedy. The Garden State's voters showed a startling reversal of their 1964 sentiment in the two subsequent elections, both of which saw New Jerseyans vote for Richard Nixon. Johnson had won the state in 1964 by a margin of 903,828 votes; Richard Nixon took New Jersey by 61,261 votes, a switch of 965,089 votes in just four years.[154] Lyndon B. Johnson would never again return to New Jersey—just like he would never again return to the level of popularity and exuberance that was on display in Paramus in 1964. In many ways, New Jersey would also never return to the same excitement levels when seeing its commander in chief. The presidencies of Johnson and Nixon (with his scandals) would see to it that the American people would never again fully trust their leaders in Washington. The Johnsonmania of 1964 became a moment suspended in a time of lost innocence. It was not seen in America again until perhaps the massive rallies of President Donald J. Trump—which incidentally never reached the fervor of Johnson's in New Jersey on that October morning in 1964.

8

REAGAN WOOS NEW JERSEY

R eagan is the most popular figure in the history of the United States," proclaimed Speaker of the House Tip O'Neill on the day of the president's 1984 reelection win. "No candidate we put up would have been able to beat Reagan this year."[155] Exaggeration? Perhaps. But not without merit. Ronald Reagan, the fortieth president of the United States, was generally well-liked by the American people. Based on Gallup Poll ratings that measured the public's personal opinion rather than the assessment of his job, between 1982 and 1988, 74 percent of Americans had a favorable opinion of Reagan as a person, even during the 1982 recession, when only about four in ten Americans approved of what he was doing.[156] A recent 2021 Newsweek article summed up Ronald Reagan as a "decent and temperate man who chose his words carefully," adding that he was "the most successful president of the last half-century, in terms of putting ideas into practice" and always made people feel comfortable around him. People liked his demeanor, humor, humility and friendliness, even if they did not always like his policies. By the time of President Regan's numerous visits to New Jersey in his bid for reelection in 1984, the onetime Hollywood actor had already captured the hearts and imaginations of the American people. Looking back at his visits now in the 2020s, it becomes almost impossible to imagine a time when politics were still civil, and people could separate the person from their brand, a time of a Hollywood president, literally and figuratively.

A poster for the Reagan-Bush 1984 campaign. *Library of Congress.*

Opponents called him the "Teflon president" because it seemed like nothing negative could stick to him. His supporters countered with the moniker of "the great communicator." In reality, he was somewhere in the middle—loved by some, hated by others, and liked by most. Historian Eric Foner would say, "Reagan made conservatism seem progressive, rather than an attempt to turn back the tide of progress."[157] Following his 1980 election, the onetime California governor cut taxes, reduced social spending, and placed greater reliance on the state, local, and community efforts.[158] There is no denying that during his administration, the United States' economy witnessed the longest peacetime expansion in its history. Still, it also caused record budget deficits to achieve this. Reagan was less popular with the left for severely cutting social spending in favor of higher military budgets and for lacking environmental sentiment. Reagan offset his cuts in youth training, school lunches and food stamps by strengthening the American military position. His administration reopened negotiations with the Soviet Union and brought the two nations closer to ending the long-running Cold War. Somehow, while the people disagreed about his policies, they could not always agree on whether they liked or disliked him—he was simply Ronald Reagan.

It was Reagan's personality that seemed to mesmerize the public the most. This was further exacerbated when a mentally unstable man shot him in the spring of 1981. His ability to joke with the doctors when he was being wheeled into the operating room with a bleeding gunshot wound (when he famously told them he hoped they were all Republican) only further endeared him in the hearts of the American people. Any official or unofficial visit by the American president is a celebration, but a visit from Reagan transcended them all; it truly was a visit by the most popular man in America, if not the world. People looked forward to seeing the president in their state and especially looked forward to hearing him speak. The so-called great communicator, with his positive and quiet demeanor, utilized the dominant media of his generation, the television, to play up his celebrity status by speaking directly to the American people without a filter. But it was when he was on the campaign trail that he shined. He loved talking to people.

It did not matter to him whether you were a successful businessman or a clerk at a food market. There was a certain sincerity to him that people who met him spoke of feeling. Often, when he was back in his car or on the presidential airplane, he would turn to his aid and say, "There was a man back there who…" proceeding to describe someone's plight and asking what he could do to help them.[159] He loved campaigning, not strictly to pass on his political agenda, but also to meet people. He was known as a jokester, an animated person, and an entertainer of sorts, something attributed to his acting background. Reagan was even known to become friendly with his political adversaries. And while calling it a friendship would be an overstatement, his relationship with Democratic Speaker of the House O'Neill certainly displayed that this was a time when people could disagree politically and still communicate as people. The speaker was known to have said extremely negative things about the president in public. According to the Reagan Foundation, Reagan had a rule that all negative speech regarding each other should stop at 6:00 p.m., when the politics would stop, and they could talk person to person.[160] Ultimately, the great communicator and his political opponent worked out numerous significant compromises on taxes, Social Security, welfare, immigration and national defense budgets.

When it was time to run a reelection campaign in 1984, which would see the popular president visit the Garden States three times in two months, his popularity rating was the highest of any commander in chief since Dwight D. Eisenhower. And just like Ike, who had, up to that point, been the oldest president to serve when he stepped down at the age of seventy, Reagan faced the same attacks of agism, pointing to the fact that if reelected, he would be seventy-six. Regardless of the pushback toward his conservative deregulation policies, deficits and welfare cuts, the "age issue" became the center of the new campaign. From the opposition's standpoint, it made sense to go after the man and not his policies, which, although unpopular with about half of the nation, paled in comparison to President Reagan's general respect. Soon, the news was full of the president's erratic behaviors, which questioned his vigor and ability to serve another four years. Comments of Reagan falling asleep in cabinet meetings were only further supplemented by some stumbling behavior in public appearances. During the first of two televised debates with his opponent, the former vice president under Carter, Walter Mondale, the president seemed to draw a blank and then ramble off-topic. The *Wall Street Journal* was not too kind: "Is the Oldest U.S. President Now Showing His Age?" asked the headline—"Reagan debate performance invites open speculation on his ability to serve."[161]

Forever the entertainer, Reagan once again proved his moniker as a "Teflon president" when he recovered ground and confidence at the following debate with perhaps some of his most famous words: "I will not make age an issue of this campaign," he stated. "I'm not going to exploit for political purposes my opponent's youth and inexperience."[162] Yet these accusations of old age promoted Reagan to campaign vigorously, especially in important swing states such as New Jersey, even though there was no doubt of his eventual win among his constituents. The Garden State found itself a vital campaign stop in the 1984 election, beginning with the Democratic primaries, one of the more intense and contentious primaries until 2008, which pitted Hilary Clinton against the eventual winner, Barrack Obama.

The eight-way race narrowed down to Colorado senator Gary Hart, Chicago civil rights activist Reverend Jesse Jackson and former vice president Walter F. Mondale of Minnesota. Both Walter Mondale and Gary Hart called "New Jersey's primary election crucial in their pursuit of the Democratic presidential nomination."[163] Both pledged to spend as much time as would be needed to get all the delegates needed, with Mondale making a record for a primary: eleven visits to the state. Hart made four visits, and Jackson courted the state's extensive Black population on two occasions. Mondale, who appealed to the Garden State's vast senior citizen and union member population, was not too forthcoming when he took the time in the state to campaign not just against his Democratic opponents but against the American president as well. On June 5, 1984, after a long and tiresome campaign, New Jersey's 107 delegates concurred with the rest of the nation and picked Mondale for the Democratic ticket. By then, even the new Democratic candidate was calling the campaign glacial.

The Reagan administration wasted no time in countering Mondale in New Jersey, a state which the Associated Press labeled a "battleground" and "the state regarded as key to presidential victory."[164] According to the independent global news organization, both parties' leaders predicted that the candidate who won New Jersey in November would also win the presidency. "New Jersey is vital, absolutely vital to both candidates," said Republican governor Thomas H. Kean, adding, "Whoever wins New Jersey wins the presidency. It's that simple." The Democratic state chairman James Maloney called the Garden State "the pivotal state in the Northeast."[165] Reagan wasted no time and launched his campaign in New Jersey barely a week after the Democrats chose Walter F. Mondale as their candidate. It was not lost on those running the Republican campaign that the New Jersey delegation pushed Mondale over the top in the count of delegates needed for his nomination.[166] As much as the Republicans denied it, the media saw Reagan's barrage of visits to the northern state as a counter to Mondale's recent growth in the polls. "We're not responding to the Mondale-Ferraro ticket. We're just campaigning in a state that is essential for the president's re-election," said Representative James Courter (R-NJ), Reagan's state campaign chairman.[167] So, Reagan was ready to come to New Jersey to once again concentrate on working-class and ethnic areas that gave him support in 1980 while simultaneously courting independent, blue-collar Democrats.

As far as the news outlets were concerned, this visit from Reagan was a noncampaigning visit. Yet the president managed to address one of the more concerning domestic issues when he stopped over at River Dell High School in Oradell on Wednesday, June 20, 1984; it was the first of three visits leading up to the November election. The short and more intimate-in-nature-event at a local high school fit nicely with Reagan's image of being a personable leader and did just enough to garner attention in the important swing state. One thousand teenagers wildly greeted the president as he showed up to speak about drunk driving dangers and shifted his stance on supporting a new national mandate of an "age-21" drinking law. A bill sponsored by a Democratic New Jersey senator, Frank Lautenberg, proposed withholding 5 percent of a state's federal highway money if it chose not to adhere to a

Ronald Reagan speaking to about nine hundred students at River Dell High School about the problems of drinking and driving. *Photographer: Jack Anderson;* Herald News *(Passaic, NJ), June 21, 1984.*

suggested twenty-one minimum drinking age. While it was approved in the House, the Senate debated the bill. To the surprise of many, the Reagan administration reversed its course and decided to back the nonpartisan proposal. It was time to make that stance official, and there was no better place or perhaps more important place to do so than in the state from which the proposal originated and which the Republicans needed to court.

The students and faculty were ecstatic by the visit from arguably one of the most famous American presidents of all time, all while Republican news networks loved the media opportunity to highlight their leader's humility. Reagan shook hands with the overwhelmed teenagers before posing for pictures behind the wheel of a driving simulator and eventually addressing the student body. He praised the Garden State for its campaign to curtail drunk driving. The great communicator acknowledged that his decision may appear to be "at odds with my philosophical viewpoint that state problems should involve state solutions." Yet as the president pointed out to the cheering crowd, "drunk driving is more than just a state problem. It is a national tragedy involving transit across state borders…which we just

President Reagan sits behind the wheel of a driving simulator during a visit to River Dell Regional High School in Oradell, New Jersey. *Daily Register (Red Bank, NJ), June 21, 1984.*

can't tolerate anymore."[168] He proceeded to praise New Jersey for being the first to raise its drinking age to twenty-one in 1983 and pointed to the 26 percent reduction in nighttime vehicular accidents among teenagers. In a charismatic and equally upbeat and somber speech that resembled a defense of a political agenda, mixed with parenting advice, Reagan highlighted the problem of students driving to nearby states where the drinking age was younger and then coming back across state lines while driving under the influence.

A quadriplegic student from Dover gave a moving speech about the drunk driving accident that resulted in his paralysis: "I can't move my fingers, but I'm ready to shake the hand of the president of the United States of America."[169] Reagan walked over to the young man and gripped his hand as others joined him in a standing ovation. The event concluded with a somber Reagan turning his attention to the teenagers in the audience: "As a man who has lived seventy-three years and who has seen a lot, I just want to tell you: don't take drugs....Don't fall for that stuff about 'life in the fast lane'—that's where all the worst crashes are."[170] The students and faculty clapped, and the reporters who were sitting to the side marked their notepads, surely a winning start for President Reagan in New Jersey. The president left the gym on a happier note, as the high school jazz ensemble played Glenn Miller's "In the Mood," a private request of Reagan, who asked for more upbeat 1930s and 1940s music instead of the traditional "Hail to the Chief."

Passaic's *Herald News* pointed out how "the tight security, hundreds of reporters and television cameras and the sheer majesty of the president's arrival and takeoff seemed to astound many observers."[171] The same article stated that those teens who did get to meet the president personally said they were impressed "because he listened." Still, some students saw the visit for what it was. As four military helicopters readied to take the president to his next speaking engagement, the school's valedictorian told a reporter, "Reagan didn't come here for the students of River Dell; he came

President Ronald Reagan reaches from the stage to shake hands with supporters at the 1984 rally at Elizabeth City Hall. Home News *(New Brunswick, NJ), July 27, 1984.*

here for the country." He explained how the trip would give the president valuable publicity in New Jersey and across the nation.[172] One of the thirty nuclear freeze advocates who gathered with signs on the outskirts of the school property commented that he supported the school's efforts to stop drunk driving but said he resented Reagan for "using it for an election, your ploy."[173] None of that mattered to the one thousand teenagers who watched the military helicopter take off from their football field. The president of the United States had just come to their school, something that does not happen all that often.

Ronald Reagan would return to the Garden State a week later in a more official visit to start his reelection campaign, this time "charging directly into Democratic territory and attacking his rivals on their ground."[174] More than twenty-three thousand people cheered the president on at the GOP-sponsored rallies in Elizabeth, and another ten thousand cheered him on in Hoboken. In Elizabeth, the state's fourth-largest city, Democratic mayor

Thomas Dunn welcomed Reagan on the steps of city hall and even promised to turn against his party's nominee, Walter Mondale. The crowd, proudly proclaiming itself Italian, Cuban, Hispanic, Polish, or Portuguese through various banners and signs, interrupted Reagan twice during his thirty-minute speech with enthusiastic cheers and chants of "Reagan, Reagan, Reagan!" The stop in Elizabeth's ethnic neighborhood was predetermined based on the area's "ethnic vote," which had pushed Reagan ahead of Jimmy Carter in the previous presidential election, which he won by 399,193 votes. "There is another heartland of America," the president stated to the Elizabeth crowd. "A heartland of the streets—a place that welcomes tremendous numbers of Italians, Cubans, Puerto Ricans, Portuguese, Blacks, Irish and Polish Americans!"[175] The crowd erupted in cheers.

Reagan arrived in New Jersey to solidify his approval with the ethnic and blue-collar folks and turn some Democrats toward his side. And he seemed to accomplish all of this on his first visit. "Sometimes, party loyalty asks too much," Elizabeth mayor Dunn proclaimed, quoting the late President Kennedy, "and this is one of those times." Moments earlier, the Democrat had officially endorsed Ronald Reagan for president, pledging, "I will do everything possible to assist in his bid for re-election."[176] The speech, which was initially planned to last no more than ten minutes, was stretched to thirty minutes by the applause and chants from the motivated public. While some proclaimed their love for Reagan when interviewed by reporters, it was one particular twelve-year-old girl who summed it up best: "Reagan's cool."[177] Pleased by the many interruptions, the president abandoned his speech and began to speak from memory, feeding off the crowd's enthusiasm.

Before departing for nearby Hoboken, the president, who leaned down from his podium to shake hands with those who were lucky enough to secure their places early, made his way to his limousine past a large banner to the left of the steps from which he was speaking. "Democrats for Reagan," it proudly read. Above the podium Reagan had just left was another sign that proclaimed, "Elizabeth says Reagan, Reagan, Reagan," and "New Jersey and Ron—Perfect Together." Past the immediate crowds and in the shadow of the tree line stood those whose signs did not make the front pages of local newspapers. They read, "The Emperor Is Naked," referencing the fairy tale of a vain ruler in *The Emperor's New Clothes*, with others putting it more bluntly: "Go Back to Hollywood."[178]

In Hoboken, where Reagan appeared at the Italian American church festival honoring Saint Ann, the patron saint of Catholic women, Democratic city officials welcomed him with open arms. And once again, the Democratic

President Reagan could not get enough of the crowd at Elizabeth—nor could they get enough of him. *Photographer: Kathy Johnson; Courier News (Bridgewater, NJ), July 27, 1984.*

mayor yielded to the American president: "I am honored beyond words and have an obligation to open the city to him," said Steve Cappiello, Hoboken's longtime Democratic mayor. The crowds of presidential visits of yesteryear might have shrunk, yet the honor that came with the commander in chief's visits was far from diminished. It transcended politics. It showed respect for the office and the man who held it, regardless of the political beliefs that followed him or his opposition. Forever a charmer and an entertainer, a grinning Reagan stated, "I have no reservation about throwing my candidacy on the mercies of the good people of St. Ann's Church in Hoboken and asking them to give a kid a chance."[179] Like in Elizabeth, the crowds of people in Hoboken cheered loudly and applauded at every pause. For the many people in the audience, this was a once-in-a-lifetime event. It also did not hurt that the president was welcomed by a special guest, Frank Sinatra, who made an extremely rare appearance in his hometown. When asked about Reagan's visit after its conclusion, New Jersey governor Thomas Kean summed it up: "Any time the president comes into New Jersey, it's a chance to showcase the state," he said, adding, "[Reagan] is re-emphasizing the importance of the state, and I expect to see more of him."[180] It did not take all that long for his prediction to come true.

A poll taken by a market research firm under the sponsorship of the Asbury Park Press in early October found Reagan leading Mondale in the state, 59 percent to 25 percent. That did not stop the American president from finding enough time for one more stump through the Garden State before the big day in November.[181] Like the president's other two visits to New Jersey, this one was also full of love and recognition for him, with a little bit of anti-Reaganism sprinkled in. And although it was in no way at the level of heckling seen in the twenty-first-century elections, it was a welcome sign of American democracy at work, just as the effigy seen by Lincoln on his trip to the Garden State more than a century before had been.

Reagan arrived in Hackensack directly by helicopter, while his entourage and reporters arrived via airplane at Newark Airport on October 26, 1984. It was rainy and cold, which did not deter the two thousand who showed up at the Hackensack City Hall to hear their president speak. Although he was scheduled to appear at 5:00 p.m., the rally was delayed to wait for the arrival of the TV networks and the national press, who were still making their way from the airport. When the delay was explained to the public, many groaned and booed the reporters for making them wait, as many had stood in the uncharacteristic cold since the early morning. As an extra security precaution, everyone present had to pass through a metal detector before they were allowed into the designated area, which used construction equipment and large trucks to block off the space from surrounding streets. A Bergen County spokeswoman admitted that earlier in the day, a man with a loaded .357-caliber Magnum was arrested "exactly where the helicopter was landing."[182] The secret service stopped and questioned the man about five hours before the president's scheduled arrival and deemed it a coincidence. "He had a loaded gun, and its license had just expired," stated a special agent of the secret service, adding, "the arrest had nothing to do with the visit, and we are not pressing any charges."[183]

The president finally stepped onto the platform set up in front of the Hackensack City Hall around 5:30 p.m. and delivered "a confident, relaxed, twenty-four-minute speech, in which he promised that America's best years were ahead."[184] Directly in front of Reagan hung a mammoth of an American flag that had been hoisted on the face of the nine-story United Jersey Bank Building. In front of it and facing him was a large crowd interrupting his speech with chants of "Four more years!" The visibly delighted president stopped looking at his notes and responded with, "All right, I wasn't going to, but OK, if you insist."[185] The vigorous applause reverberated around the square. The polls were in his favor, and instead of going heavy on the offense, the president mostly stuck to his patriotic message of hope and a better tomorrow while summarizing his opponent's policies as nothing but "promises and promises." Still, this was very much Reagan. Forever the entertainer, he continued to make the crowd roar with laughter. Playing on the theme of the upcoming Halloween, he again induced laughter by saying, "If I can find a mask that looks like Mondale's plan, I can just scare the devil out of all the neighbors."[186] After many jokes, mixed with messages of a strong economy and low taxes, Reagan closed his speech with an appeal to the country's youth. He promised them that it was his duty to make sure that their America was full of opportunity, hope, confidence and dreams.

Although the small handful of hecklers who stood in the back of the crowd was not shown in the news, local newspapers picked them up. Holding signs that read "Dump Reagan, not chemicals" and "Reagan cuts kill children," the few men and women who showed up to oppose the president were drowned out by the enthusiastic crowds. "He lies to the TV camera, and he gets away with it because of his grandfatherly image people like to trust," said one of the protesters. "He didn't say one word about toxic waste; he didn't even deal with any issues."[187] The disgruntled party crashers referred to what the Eagleton Poll of Rutgers University found was New Jersey residents' number-one domestic concern in 1984: toxic waste cleanup. Dwarfing

Ronald Reagan supporters jam on Main Street in Hackensack. A mammoth U.S. flag is draped from the United Jersey Bank Building. Herald News *(Passaic, NJ), October 27, 1984.*

unemployment and inflation, the issue of the environment was a real one for Garden State, a place the *Washington Post* called "so awash in environmental problems that it has been called 'the landfill of opportunity.'"[188]

The Garden State was, at the time of Reagan's visit, home to more dangerous toxic dumps than any other state in the Union—95 to the nationwide number of 786. A few miles off the New Jersey Turnpike was a cluster of refining and petrochemical industries that generated a stew of hazardous wastes, and it was known as "Cancer Alley."[189] However, it was apparent that even the Democrats had lost all hope that any of the two candidates running for office would clean up the mess. And even though Reagan trailed far behind Mondale on environmental issues, New Jersey votes were becoming more pragmatic about the issue. One registered Democrat and environmentalist announced that she would vote for Reagan regardless of Mondale, saying he would address the issue if elected. "Everybody says they're going to clean up the rotten dump, but it has been here through Democrats and Republicans," she said.[190] These views were on full display in Hackensack on October 26, 1984, when Reagan came to town. According to a local poll, most "on-the-fence" New Jerseyans who supported Carter in 1976 said, "they will now vote for Reagan because they believe he is better for their pocketbooks."[191] At the time of Reagan's visit, the Garden State witnessed industry growth not seen since World War II, with the unemployment rate dropping to 6 percent, well below the national average. On November 6, Ronald Reagan would take New Jersey once again.

PRESIDENT REAGAN'S INSISTENCE ON visiting the Garden State three times in the months leading up to his reelection paid off. The crowds were not at the same levels they were for Teddy Roosevelt, Franklin Roosevelt or even Lyndon B. Johnson, yet Reagan still managed to capture the imaginations of the people of New Jersey. More importantly, he managed to capture their votes. Reagan carried the state with 60.09 percent of the vote to his opponent's 39.20 percent, a margin of slightly over 20 percent.[192] Yet that was not all. The incumbent president nearly repeated Johnson's feat from twenty years before: winning every county in the state, regardless of its previous party affiliation. The only county to rebuke Regan in 1984 was Essex, with even the heavy Democratic hotbeds of Hudson County and Mercer County voting Republican, something not repeated by any other Republican running for president since.

With 1.9 million votes in New Jersey, the most received by a Republican in the state's history, Reagan seemed unstoppable.[193] In a time shaped by television and pop culture, Reagan played his part splendidly, "a masterful performer, an unabashed patriot and a champion of traditional manners and morals."[194] Historian Walter LaFaber had perhaps said it best when he alluded to the president having carried forty-nine of the fifty states in the 1984 election. "Ronald Reagan had established the terms of political debate for the 1980s as surely as Franklin Roosevelt had for the 1930s." It was dynasty and legacy that would be challenged, especially in New Jersey, in 1988 and again in 1992, with the former being the last year a Republican won the Garden State.

CLINTON TAKES OVER BUSH

t is perhaps fitting that the election of 1992 had the largest voter turnout since the 1960 election, which had one of the most charismatic candidates to ever run for the presidency in John F. Kennedy. The last decade of the twentieth century had its version of charisma and "cool" in the youngest candidate since Kennedy in William "Bill" Jefferson Clinton. One of the two hundred eighteen to twenty-four-year-olds who interviewed the Democratic candidate on an MTV-sponsored forum called him "real smooth," while another called his plan "straight-forward."[195] The dichotomy between the two candidates could not have been any greater. The incumbent president, George H.W. Bush, epitomized traditional politics and conservatism, while his younger opponent stood for a change from the right to the moderate middle. Where Bush was floundering trying to fill Reagan's shoes, the young Clinton was riding a high while appealing to the changing face of the electorate—the youth.

It did not matter that the incumbent president was perhaps the most qualified person to ever hold the office. The war hero, successful congressman, former head of the CIA, vice president and then president of the United States was unfairly seen as out of touch with the public, specifically the middle class. With the economy deep into another recession and his 1988 campaign promises about not raising taxes long ago broken, Bush had failed to match his opponent's urgency and charisma. Unlike the president, who gave speeches at expensive luncheons, Clinton took his campaign on the road to college campuses around the nation to sell his down-to-earth, middle-class, Main Street American persona. The Garden State, in 1992, was inundated with both messages—Bush's struggling conservatism and Clinton's ambitious call for a national rebirth. Like eighty years before, when Wilson faced Taft and Roosevelt, New Jersey once again became one of the most coveted and important states for the candidates. The election would become pivotal in the state's history, as it would mark the last time the Garden State played the part of an important swing state in a national election; 1992 also became the year that New Jersey turned from being a Republican shoo-in to the Democratic blue heaven it is today. It was possibly also the last time visits to the Garden State from the current and upcoming American president solicited as much excitement as they had in the past.

While Bush held a significant approval rating for the first three years of his single term as president of the United States, the year leading up to his reelection did not look promising for him. The economic expansion that followed the 1982 recession all but fizzled out by 1990, plunging the nation back into a new recession that lasted until the middle of 1991. With the start of a new decade, the economy tethered on the fence of recovery and recession, with unemployment rising to 7.5 percent. The voter paradigm set by Reagan also changed. The popular Republican president once appealed to white southerners, blue-collar workers and Catholics who traditionally identified as Democrats. Yet by 1992, surveys revealed "deep cynicism among voters toward professional politicians," with only 29 percent of the electorate expressing strong identification with either political party.[196] While Bush, perhaps due to overconfidence, ran a careless campaign that did not appeal to the "independent" voter, the younger Clinton plunged right into the people's calls for moderate leadership.

As the economy continued to show signs of imploding in early 1992, President Bush ran a campaign that focused on highlighting his foreign policy victories, while his audience, the American people, wanted a leader who addressed their struggles at the gas pumps and supermarket registers. Instead of providing the people with a credible domestic program, the Bush campaign misled its leader into believing that his reelection was all but assured by continuing to highlight his triumph against Saddam Hussain in the Gulf War from the year prior. All of a sudden, President Bush seemed aloof and out of touch with the American public, a damaging accusation—and one that may or may not have been credible—at the time when the economic hardships further pushed the commander in chief behind Clinton in the polls. A *New York Times* article, written based on a description later

Presidential nominee George H.W. Bush and his wife, Barbara Bush, wave to the crowd at the 1992 Republican National Convention in Huston, Texas. *Library of Congress.*

questioned for its validity by another journalist, described an incident on the campaign trail that solidified Bush as a leader who was out of touch with middle-class life. The article stated the president ran a few items over an electronic scanner at the grocery store and that "a look of wonder flickered across his face again as he saw the item and price registered on the cash register screen."[197] It became the biggest and most mockable out-of-touch moment in recent American politics, which sealed the president's fate. All of this was further compounded by the 1992 Los Angeles race riots that left behind $1 billion in damages, 50 dead, and another 1,500 arrested. The press was ruthless in blaming the riots on "the failure of the Reagan-Bush administrations to address the needs of the inner city." Thus, with the conservative wing of his party already turned against him after tax hikes on the wealthy and now with middle-class America doing the same, George H.W. Bush was stumbling into the ring for his bout with the young, energetic and popular Bill Clinton.

Clinton, a new Democrat and self-prescribed moderate, promised the American people historical change. The witty and intelligent candidate who would become the first president born after World War II represented a generational transfer of power, much like Kennedy had in 1960. Clinton's campaign promised cuts in the defense budget, tax relief for middle-class Americans and economic aid to former communist nations in Europe. Also, like Kennedy, whom the press often compared Clinton to, the young Democrat received staunch support among women, Black Americans, the very poor and the elderly.[198] And like Kennedy, Clinton's womanizing would attempt to put a blemish on his rising popularity, with multiple women coming forward with stories of his infidelity. In addition, Clinton earned the nickname "Slick Willie" for his inconsistency on various issues and attendance to special interest groups. The cautiously constructed responses to reporters' questions about his avoidance of the Vietnam draft and his collegiate marijuana use, which he

The 1992 official White House picture of President Bill Clinton. *Library of Congress.*

tried to explain away by saying he "didn't inhale," only added to his issues.[199]

Some people still mention in passing that MTV got Bill Clinton elected in 1992, and while that is far from the truth, the opinion does hold some merit. On its way toward making politics more relevant and appealing to America's youth, the music television channel invited the ultra-popular on college campuses, Bill Clinton, to an open forum. Politics would meet entertainment, and there was no better candidate in 1992 than the Democratic nominee when it came to entertainment. The dichotomy between Clinton and Bush could not have been more evident after the MTV forum. Appealing to the youth had been attempted before in politics, albeit without much success—until Clinton. In the televised session that lasted thirty minutes past its planned one-hour discussion, the candidate answered many of the questions posed by college students, ranging from alcohol abuse to lowering the national deficit, and spoke about the importance of listening to the nation's youth. Within a few weeks, Clinton would continue his quest for the young vote through a parade of appearances on late-night television shows, where he would famously play the saxophone while wearing stylish Ray-Ban sunglasses on the Arsenio Hall Show. He would continue his rapport with the entertainment and television audience established in 1992 when he returned to the MTV forum two years later. In a now-infamous moment, an audience member asked the president if he preferred boxers or briefs, to which the surprised and amused Clinton answered briefs. This disparity between the old and traditional politics exemplified by Bush and the new, witty, and "cool" version that Clinton embodied would collide and be prominently displayed on the campaign trail. And New Jersey would be one of its greatest benefactors.

When the Bush and Clinton campaigns began in 1992, the Garden State rode a two-decade streak of voting Republican in national elections. More importantly, it was also at the height of living up to its label as a crucial swing state. For most of the twentieth century—and apart from two presidential races—the state had swung from party to party, "perfecting the idea that as goes Jersey, so goes America."[200] During this time, New Jersey also nearly matched the nation's vote percentage for all winning candidates. Thus, it was evident for both camps that the Garden State was important to the overall outcome, especially for President George H.W. Bush, with all indicators pointing to him losing California and needing all the electoral votes he could get. According to Associated Press, the surge of new voters in New Jersey was the largest seen since Reagan's victory in 1984, a state record. However, upon closer analysis, the numbers did favor the moderate Clinton, who aimed for the undecided, independent young voters in New Jersey. Of the vast majority of the newly registered voters in the Garden State, half or approximately 270,000 people had not signed up with either major party. The two major parties split the remaining registrants, 52,561 Democrat and 52,206 Republican.[201]

As far as presidential visits go, the visit in 1992 outmatched all others before it, especially regarding the consistency of the president and his opponent in stopping by the Garden State. The news of Clinton and Bush's visits was so frequent that it nearly took away from all the glamour and honor of having them. And this showed through the announcements of the visits, now often relegated to the interior pages of newspapers. At one point, President Bush campaigned in New Jersey at a rate of once every ten days. Clinton visited the state on six different occasions, at one point telling his supporters in Jersey City a week before the election that Jersey "can turn out the lights" on the Bush presidency.[202] The Garden State proved to be significant enough to the election that both candidates spent the last day of their campaign trail stumping in New Jersey, the last time New Jersey really mattered in the national election.

President Bush and Arkansas governor Clinton jump-started their campaigning in New Jersey within days of the Democratic National

Convention in New York City on July 16, 1992. For the president, New Jersey would not extend the same rock 'n' roll welcome Johnson received in 1964. Although officially billed as a presidential event, Bush's visit to the ethnically diverse Garfield was referred to by local papers very bluntly as the first campaign stop in his re-election bid. One campaign operative plainly stated, "Unless George Bush wants to be the first GOP presidential candidate in three decades to lose New Jersey, he'll have to visit the state frequently and campaign furiously, as if he were running for a state office, not the nation's highest post."[203] It was no coincidence that Bush decided to visit the Garden State so soon after the announcement of Clinton as his opponent. New Jersey's opinion polls had the president twenty-five points behind the charismatic governor of Arkansas.

Flags from forty different countries flew around the podium that was set up on the steps of Garfield's Three Saints Russian Orthodox Church on July 21, 1992. The six-thousand-strong crowd gathered in the sweltering heat hours before the scheduled talk. As everyone waited for the president's arrival, six performance groups representing different countries and cultures, including Wallington's Polish National Alliance Dancers, entertained the crowd, which filled the church parking lot. There were signs everywhere, some favorable and others not so much. The abortion issue seemed to be front and center, with giant banners reading "Keep Abortion Legal" and "Stop Abortion Now," as well as "No Bush! We Don't Have a Choice!" While one group held a banner proclaiming "We Love George Bush," another, just yards away, stated, "No More Bush!" The more than fifty-five city police officers and an undisclosed number of secret service agents and the special officers manning the metal detectors set up around the parking lot could not prevent a scuffle that started within the crowd. Four young men who called themselves anarchists burned and then trampled on an American flag. When a World War II veteran stepped up to grab the burning flag, he was promptly shoved, resulting in others entering the fray and throwing punches.

Bush stepped up to the platform at 3:30 p.m., minutes after police broke up the fight in the crowd. From the onset, the president was all business. Apart from a few waves, Bush's only acknowledgement of the crowd was a smile to one person who was holding a sign that read, "Bush/Quayle will prevail."[204] Instead of speaking on the economy, which the polls showed to be the most crucial issue, Bush played to his strengths and his ethnically diverse crowd and spoke about the fall of communism and his successful foreign policy. This paid dividends with the mostly Polish, Italian, German, and Russian crowd. The president's biggest cheer came after he proclaimed that the communist Castro dictatorship in Cuba was on its last legs, promising that he would personally visit the small island nation within the next four years.

As Bush continued with his thirty-minute speech, at least four people were evacuated from the premises and treated for illnesses related to hot weather.[205] Due to his delayed arrival, many of the patrons had left early to avoid the unbearable heat, and more would do so after the volunteers ran out of the cold water bottles they had been handing out all afternoon. At one point, a young preteen who was wearing a Clinton hat was overheard booing the president, which got another person angry. "Shut up, you little jerk," said the red-faced guy. "We came to listen to the president, not to you." Another person holding a "Read my lips: No second term" sign promptly joined the fray in heckling the angry man. In the end, Bush failed to make an impression on New Jersey during his first unofficial campaign stop. The diminishing crowds, a large number of hecklers and his own reluctance to speak about domestic issues made the visit one of the least memorable visits of any American president to the Garden State. One Garfield man who attended the speech did not mince any words: "He is a good man, believe me, but he has to do something about the economy….I am worse off than I was four years ago." He then added what many people were likely feeling: "If Bush would've been here four years ago, I wouldn't have been able to come; I would have been working. But work is slow, so I'm here."[206]

Clinton's first stop in New Jersey, which was a bit quieter than that of his Republican adversary, occurred just a few days earlier. Instead of a big presidential rally—after all, he was still a mere candidate—Clinton chose the Garden State's Camden as the start of his eight-state bus trip to the heartland of the United States. Fresh from their victory at the Democratic National Convention in New York, Clinton and his running mate, Al Gore's, bus stopped at the General Electric aerospace plant on Camden's waterfront on July 18, 1992. The five hundred or so plant employees listened attentively as the young Democrat promised to return the government to the people. Hundreds of additional supporters who were waving signs gathered outside to see the candidates off on their journey. While this was by no means a presidential visit—and one that paled even in comparison to Bush's lackluster showing in Garfield—there was a lot of symbolism and cunning planning involved in Clinton starting his campaign in New Jersey's Camden. There was not a better place in the United States that the Clinton-Gore ticket could point to as the epitome of Bush's economic policy failure. Once a major industrial center, Camden was New Jersey's poorest city. A *TIME* magazine article had, just a few months before, called it "a run-down, burned-out sinkhole where no one would choose to live." At the time of Clinton's stop, nearly half of the city's eighty-seven thousand residents lived on public assistance, and more than half of its children lived in poverty.[207]

The September 1992 Bush and Clinton visits to the Garden State highlighted the differing approaches of the candidates' campaigns and their diverging results. First came Clinton's visit to Rahway on September 24, where he detailed his healthcare plan to about 1,500 supporters at Merck & Co. Inc. The visit was a standard fare for the candidate, with smiles, handshakes, applause, and a handful of hecklers. Some college students took it upon themselves to shout, "White House, not whorehouse," and "No Slick Willie" at the presidential candidate.[208] They were soon escorted off the premises. Perhaps the most memorable part of the campaign stop came courtesy of a four-month-old infant. Clinton picked up the baby, who was sporting an "I'm a Democrat, and I love it!' pin, only for the infant to vomit on the lapel of his blue jacket. "I don't mind," Clinton said with a laugh as he moved along to shake more hands. "That's what babies do."[209] Clinton was just charming the New Jersey crowds, and they were beginning to warm up to him.

Apart from a short speech, in which the president of the United States addressed a small contingent of four hundred working women on family leave plans at the AT&T corporate headquarters in Basking Ridge, not much else happened in terms of campaigning until the last day of the month, September 30. The day brought both candidates back to the Garden State, and their approaches to campaigning could not have been more different. While the president chose to adhere to his old-school politics of courting unions— in this case, the construction union workers at Newark's union hall in the city's Ironbound District—Clinton instead opted for the younger crowds of Drew University in Madison. For Bush, this was once again a whimper of a visit compared to the grandeur that once accompanied American presidents when they came to town. It was the commander in chief's fifth appearance in the Garden State. He arrived at Newark International Airport, where the Newark Policeman's Benevolent Association and the New Jersey Fraternal Oder of Police welcomed him with a small ceremony that lasted less than fifteen minutes. Unlike the visits of Teddy Roosevelt or even Ike, where thousands of people lined up for the presidential motorcade, the president did not go through towns but instead took the two-mile stretch of the New Jersey Turnpike closed to all other traffic. His motorcade made its way to the union hall of Heavy and General Construction Laborers' Local 472.[210]

Left: Presidential candidate Bill Clinton embracing fellow Democrat governor Jim Florio after giving a healthcare speech at Merk & Co. in Rahway on September 24, 1992. Daily Record *(Morristown, NJ), September 25, 1992.*

Right: Democratic presidential candidate Bill Clinton holding a four-month-old toddler during a campaign appearance in Rahway. The baby vomited on the lapel of his suit jacket. Record *(Hackensack, NJ), September 25, 1992.*

Five hundred people gave the president a very raucous reception, with chants of "Four more years!" His short speech homed in on Clinton's draft record and his performance as the governor of Arkansas, while offering little on the national economy. However, Bush managed to get loud cheers when he spoke of family values, his World War II military record and his successes in battling the Cold War. Outside and securely behind police barriers stood about one hundred or so protesters, with anti-Bush signs held high. One memorable banner read, "You're No Harry Truman," referring to President Bush comparing himself to Truman during his party's nomination acceptance speech; Truman, like himself, faced a time of uncertainty in the nation. The president attempted to compare himself to the late Truman by evoking the 1948 whistle-stop railroad tour across the nation. The former president successfully took his reelection bid directly to the American people and won against all odds. Unfortunately, the same magic that worked for Truman would not strike twice to help the elder Bush.

Above: Governor Bill Clinton speaking to the press at the Garden State Exhibit Center in Franklin. Courier News *(Bridgewater, NJ), October 1, 1992.*

Right: President Bush addresses construction workers at a Newark union hall in September 1992. Courier News *(Bridgewater, NJ), October 1, 1992.*

Opposite: Newspapers had a field day when President Bush and Governor Clinton both visited New Jersey on the same day to speak to much different crowds. *Left*: Bush meeting with several police groups. *Right*: Clinton speaking to college students at Drew University. Home News *(New Brunswick, NJ), October 1, 1992.*

President Bush thrusts his fists upward yesterday as he greets supporters at Newark International Airport, where he got the backing of several police groups.

Democratic presidential candidate Bill Clinton, speaking at Drew University, says he would be willing to join President Bush on the "Larry King Live" show Sunday.

Bush lumps Clinton, Florio

President: Foe would up taxes on middle class

MORE STORIES
- Perot continued to fund campaign after dropping out
- Bush, Clinton, Perot compete for air time on morning shows
— Stories on Page A8 —

Dem challenger offers to join president on TV

By AUDREY KELLY
Home News Trenton bureau

FRANKLIN — Looking to regain the high ground in the tumult surrounding the elusive presidential debates, Bill Clinton

White House for the first time in 12 years.
Clinton told the crowd at the convention center that he expects them to work hard during the final 34 days of the campaign. "You have to help America and New Jersey keep its courage up," Clinton said. "The oth-

That same day across the state, Bill Clinton spoke to an enthusiastic crowd of college students at Drew University. The entire event took an unexpected twist on September 30, 1992. Clinton was scheduled to arrive at Morristown Municipal Airport for a small rally before departing for his larger stop at the Garden State Convention and Exhibition Center (Somerset). Fearing the Clinton crowds and the disruption they would cause to the traffic patterns in and around Morristown, the airport management called the Clinton campaign manager the night before his scheduled arrival to cancel the small rally. The airport stated it could not accommodate the anticipated number of persons who were coming in to see the Democratic candidate. Not having anywhere to go before his big Exhibition Center gala, where more than two thousand people had paid $1,500 for a chance to wine and dine with Clinton, the presidential candidate turned to his old friend and then-president of Drew University, a former Republican governor and then chairman of Bush's New Jersey campaign, Tom Kean.[211]

In a turn of events that seems very unlikely to happen in today's world of partisan politics, Kean offered Clinton his university campus to hold a rally. At the same time, he could not attend the rally, as he was hosting the American president in Newark at the same time. "The nation faces a choice

Bill Clinton speaking to college students at Drew University in September 1992. Daily Record *(Morristown, NJ), October 1, 1992.*

between two outstanding candidates," Kean said in a letter read to the Drew crowd of over one thousand students before Clinton's speech. "Right now, I am in Newark meeting with the other one," continued the letter, eliciting at first laughs, then boos. "You are a good friend, and I'm sorry that I cannot be here to greet you…but want to wish you all the best."[212] Playing up to his young crowd and his "cool" factor, Clinton used the rally to call on Bush to change the proposed debate dates. "The president offered four dates that seem impractical because they're during the World Series and *Monday Night Football*."[213] He then suggested meeting on *Larry King Live*, the late-night talk show, instead, which the Bush campaign firmly rejected. The Democratic candidate got loud cheers at the conclusion of his speech, as he once again appealed to the college students in front of him. "I do not want to be part of the first generation of Americans to do worse than your parents."[214] That very evening, in more formal wear and with a more formal demeanor, Bill Clinton cajoled a much larger crowd as they dined on a five-star dinner and dessert while a jazz band played lightly in the background. In many ways, Clinton's last September day in New Jersey was much better for him than it was for his opponent, as it left a good impression on his potential voters.

President George Bush swipes at a pestering bee as he addresses a rally at Middlesex County College in Edison in October 1992. Bush joked that the fly was probably a Democrat. *Courier News (Bridgewater, NJ), October 17, 1992.*

The president and his opponent would again visit the state come October, and this time, George H.W. Bush would take a page from Clinton's book by staging a rally at the Middlesex County College. And once again, this would not be the day for the World War II hero and then-incumbent president. It was a meager showing of less than one thousand college students, especially considering that this trip was well planned and advertised, unlike Clinton's visit to Drew a couple of weeks prior. It also showed how something that was once so important for the town, the state and the people no longer was. Gone were the well-wishers, the members of opposing parties who came out to support their nation's leader, the women and children who came out in masses to wave American flags out of respect for the highest office. Instead, the glamour and jubilance that came to define the presidential visits of the past were then replaced with scenes of college kids and Clinton supporters interrupting Bush's seventeen-minute speech. The shouts of "liar" and "No more Bush!" seemed to fluster the president. "I wish these draft dodgers would shut up so I can finish my speech," proclaimed the agitated Bush, whose agitation was made obvious by the fact that the draft had ended twenty years prior.[215] Apart from the hecklers before him, the president also had to be content with a bee that kept pestering him when he addressed the crowd. Bush played up that the bee was probably a Democrat to make light of the situation. The joke failed to warm up the crowd.

Apart from Clinton's brief stop in Jersey City to speak out about battling AIDS and the subsequent hour-long live broadcast from New Jersey on October 29, the two candidates would not return to the Garden State for any meaningful appearances until just before the November election. Once again, the dichotomy between the two political opponents was on full display. Yet perhaps more importantly, it was here, at the last political stop of the last election where New Jersey truly mattered in national politics, that people saw the future of politics. Namely, they saw its final turnover—long coming—from mostly serious and respected public servitude to

Above: President Bush telling his hecklers in Edison that he wished "the draft dodgers would shut up." Daily Record *(Morristown, NJ), October 17, 1992.*

Left: President Bush shouts back at hecklers during a speech at Middlesex County College in Edison while his supporters look on. Home News *(New Brunswick, NJ), October 17, 1992.*

Opposite, left: President Bush addressing a very mixed crowd at Middlesex County College. Daily Journal *(Vineland, NJ), October 17, 1992.*

Opposite, right: A Rutgers University student wearing a Pinocchio nose heckles President Bush during his rally in Edison. Home News *(New Brunswick, NJ), October 17, 1992.*

entertainment. In a sense, the traditional politics of George H.W. Bush gave way to the more modern methods of courting the masses, and the result ultimately led to Bush's defeat. Knowing the importance of the state, Bill Clinton chose New Jersey for the last event of his Democratic campaign, a huge November 1 rally that mixed politics and entertainment at the New Jersey Meadowlands 15,600-person Brendan Byrne Arena. Fleetwood Mac, Barbara Streisand, Michael Bolton and other Grammy-winning trumpeters and musicians entertained the lucky supporters who received tickets. Then came Hollywood and Broadway appearances from Glenn Close, Richard Gere, Kathleen Turner, Gregory Hines and the entire cast of *Les Miserables*.[216]

The next day, George H.W. Bush gave his last speech in New Jersey as president of the United States at a rally in Madison. A couple thousand supporters turned out to see the president speak from the stairs of the town hall. Yet the writing was on the wall. Even the state's youth called it when

92: THE RECORD STUDENT STRAW POLL

CLINTON WINS ONE

Perot runs second, Bush trails

By JEFF SIMMONS
Record Staff Writer

A lthough most of them aren't old enough to vote on Tuesday, students in North Jersey overwhelmingly endorsed Gov. Bill Clinton for president in a straw poll conducted by The Record.

More than 55,000 high school and middle school students in Bergen and Passaic counties cast ballots in The Record Student Straw Poll in the past 10 days, with 44 percent endorsing Clinton. Texas billionaire Ross Perot was picked by 26 percent and President Bush by 24 percent.

Clinton captured 103 of 148 schools that participated in the poll. Overall, Clinton received 24,403 votes, Perot 14,253, and Bush 13,489.

Some 2,927 students checked a box on the ballot sheet indicating they would not vote for any of the three candidates.

Although only a small number of students who participated can vote in Tuesday's election, educators stressed the value of mock balloting in providing curriculum fodder while promoting debate among youths and their parents.

"This is a way to tap current interest and teach a permanent skill," said state Commissioner of Education John Ellis. The United States has "an abysmal record" of low voter turnout, said Ellis, adding, "We need to start students early to learn about their obligation to vote."

"For many students, the mock election is the first formal introduction into the democratic

❝A lot of Clinton's ideas appeal to the young generation.❞
— Robin Gwiazdowski, 15, Bogota

❝I think Perot will do what's best for the deficit and the economy.❞
— Jordana Ende, 12, Cresskill

❝Bush is more honest than Clinton, and he knows what he wants.❞

KLAUS-PETER STEITZ/THE RECORD
Bill Clinton, in a speech at the Hudson County Courthouse on Thursday, pledging his support for a national war against AIDS.

Emotional Clinton urges war on AIDS

Jersey City speech a bold but risky move

Above: The *Record* newspaper's student straw poll had Clinton winning the presidency a week before the national election. *Right*: Clinton speaks at the Hudson County Courthouse for a national war against AIDS. Record *(Hackensack, NJ), October 30, 1992.*

Opposite: Actor Richard Gere warms up the crowd at a Clinton rally held at the Meadowlands on November 1, 1992. Courier-Post *(Camden, NJ), November 2, 1992.*

the mock election held at six hundred schools across the state on the eve of the national presidential election showed New Jersey's youth giving 41 percent of their vote to Clinton. President Bush received about 30 percent, and millionaire Ross Perot, who ran independently, received 29 percent.[217] The results were even more skewed toward the Democratic candidate in the *Record* newspaper's student straw poll, which saw Clinton receive 24,403 votes to Bush's 13,489. On November 3, 1992, Bill Clinton became the first Democrat since Lyndon B. Johnson in 1964 to win New Jersey, and he did so by beating out President Bush by a slight 2.37-percent margin.

THE 1992 PRESIDENTIAL ELECTION was important to New Jersey in many ways. For one, it brought to the state a president and a future president more times in a short period than it ever had before or since. At no point in American history did the Garden State host a president ten times in three months—nor the future president in nearly the same manner for that matter. It was only the third time that New Jersey had voted Democratic since World War II, and it was the start of a Democrat winning the state by more than a ten-point margin ever since—apart from John Kerry in 2004, who won with a margin of around 7 percent. From the context of presidential visits, the election showed the diminishing excitement that the executive office carried. Gone were the crowds of supporters who waited night and day to catch a glimpse of the American president, the hundreds of thousands who packed city streets to see Teddy Roosevelt or his cousin Franklin. It would not be until President Donald Trump held a rally in front of over seven thousand supporters in Wildwood, New Jersey, on a cold day in late January 2020 that a president drew the huge numbers of supporters once seen in the Garden State for a presidential stop. By then, New Jersey had become a sort of "given" for the Democratic Party and no longer mattered enough for the leaders of either party to campaign in extensively. The 1992 election, in which the president of the United States saw the Garden State as important enough to barrage it with his presence over and over again, is now but a memory of a time when New Jersey really mattered in national politics.

TWENTY-FIRST CENTURY

FROM GEORGE W. TO BIDEN

The presidential visits to New Jersey that have taken place in the early twenty-first century are best described as small, divisive and lacking any glamor of yesteryear. In fact, apart from George W. Bush's Republican fundraiser in Edison in May 2007 and President Trump's rally in Wildwood in January 2020, the remainder of the presidential visits were associated with natural disasters and were hence smaller and more intimate. The visits also exhibited modern politics' more personal, combative and divisive nature. That is not to say that personal mudslinging had not been part of the American political arena from the onset. The 1800 election witnessed Thomas Jefferson be accused of having sex with his enslaved women—which he did—while Andrew Jackson's opponents in 1824 labeled his wife as an adulteress and him as immoral for having courted her while she was still married to another man. The New Jersey assembly openly mocked Abe Lincoln for his appearance. Later, in 1884, newspapers plastered their front pages with stories of Grover Cleveland's illegitimate child with a much younger woman. Questioning the opposite party was on full display in the 1930s, when the press referred to Roosevelt as a power-abusing monarch, and again in the 1970s against Gerald Ford, who was accused of corrupt backdoor politics when he pardoned his predecessor, Richard Nixon. The partisan politics that often accompanied presidential visits to New Jersey in the early twenty-first century were simply exacerbated by societal paradigm shifts and the pattern of society-altering events. It was a time of the September 11, 2001 attacks, the election of the first Black president and the Trump administration's ultimate fusion of media and power.

It would be pointless to try to argue against the fact that the terrorist attacks of September 11, 2001, on the United States altered all aspects of American society, especially how people's views changed on freedom, democracy and, finally, the American government. Following the attack, the American people did what they had traditionally done in times of crisis: they looked to their leadership for answers. In his address to Congress on September 20, 2001, the recently elected president George W. Bush announced a new war on terrorism, beginning with targeting al-Qaeda, responsible for the September 11 attacks, and continuing to wage war against any state that aided or supported international terrorist groups.

Within a month of the attacks, the United States launched a war in Afghanistan with the intent of bringing down the Taliban regime, which protected al-Qaeda and its leader Osama bin Landen. The Taliban government had collapsed by the year's end, and bin Laden went into hiding. And while the American people mostly supported the war, the subsequent 2003 invasion of Iraq (a nation the Republican administration claimed was hiding weapons of mass destruction with ill intent toward the west) became a turning point for George W. Bush. With the evidence against Iraq and its dictator, Saddam Hussain, possessing these weapons being circumstantial at best—and later proven to be altogether false—the American president was soon facing a strong antiwar sentiment at home. At times, it rivaled Johnson's experience in the 1960s with anti–Vietnam War opposition. The war quickly proved to be costly. Over three thousand American soldiers lost their lives within the first three years of the conflict. In fiscal terms, according to an article by *Business Insider*, the war would end up costing the nation over $2 trillion.[218]

By the time prisoner mistreatment at the American detention centers of Abu Ghraib and Guantanamo Bay became front-page news in 2004, President Bush's approval ratings were already on a steep decline. The people resented the increased domestic surveillance by the National Security Agency as part of the war on terror. Then there was a public denunciation of what the citizenry perceived as the federal government's failed response to Hurricane Katrina, which smashed into the Gulf Coast in August 2005. The pendulum had swung against the nonpartisan politics that followed the September 11 attacks. Gone were the times of Reagan, when people were able to separate the man from his party or his policies. In a phenomenon that historians and political scientists are still studying, the nation shifted toward divisive politics. With this shift, gone were nonpartisan presidential visits, for which people turned out in awe to see the president of the United States. One would be more likely to see a heckler holding a negative sign instead of a woman holding a baby waving a flag in their little hands. Similarly, gone was the impartial press; in fact, the media did not attempt to hide its own bias. By the time President Bush came to visit New Jersey on May 30, 2007, one year before the end of his term and months away from the biggest financial crisis the public had seen since the Great Depression, the opposition was all but inevitable.

Bush's visit to the New Jersey Convention and Exposition Center, where he spoke about taxes and terrorism, drew a crowd of seven hundred and raised nearly $650,000 for the Republican Party. The number was not that shocking, considering that each person attending had to pay $300 for their ticket, with an option of having a picture taken with the president for an additional $5,000. One lucky five-year-old's grandmother paid the large sum to allow her grandson to have a picture with the commander in chief that he could share in his kindergarten class's show-and-tell. Bush used the platform, where he was initially asked to show support for state Republicans running in the midterm elections, to reaffirm his commitment to winning the war in Iraq. The GOP was in a lot of trouble in the Garden State in the early 2000s, and it needed a boost afforded by a presidential visit to try to keep up with the Democrats' fundraising. According to the state's Election Law Enforcement Commission, the Garden State Democrats had raised $17 million since the beginning of 2007 for the year's legislative elections (compared to the Republicans' $7.5 million).[219]

As Bush entered the room for his speech that was to last twenty-seven minutes, an excited crowd greeted the president. The state Republican Committee chairman called them "seven hundred real Republicans and not the pay-to-play crowd you see at Democratic fundraisers."[220] A woman in the front aisle yelled, "I love you!" Bush smiled. "I love you, too," he said. The rest of the speech remained very consistent, dealing with terrorism and taxes. The president's comments about defeating the terrorists and always being on the offensive drew the fiercest applause. "You must treat them as they are—cold-blooded killers—and bring them to justice!" exclaimed Bush at one point to the many cheers around the room. Unlike in the past, where any visit by the commander in chief to a state called for a welcome by the incumbent governor—as was the case in previous New Jersey visits—the Garden State's Democratic governor Jon S. Corzine did not come out to see

Above: President George W. Bush arrives at Newark Liberty Airport for a Republican Party fundraiser in Edison on May 30, 2007. Home News Tribune *(New Brunswick, NJ)*, *May 31, 2007.*

Opposite: President Bush speaking at a Republican fundraiser at the New Jersey Convention and Exposition Center in Edison. Home News Tribune *(New Brunswick, NJ)*, *May 31, 2007.*

him. "I hope he has a fine stay in the state," Corzine said on record, "I don't wish him well in his fundraising efforts."[221]

Yet this presidential visit to New Jersey would be made more memorable by the crowd of nearly two hundred people outside the convention center. As the presidential limousine arrived in the parking lot at 5:00 p.m., loud chants against Bush rang out from the crowd. "Hey, Bush. We know you—you're a thief, a liar and a killer, too!" When the president exited his vehicle, escorted inside by the secret service, a retired schoolteacher screamed obscenities at him while holding a sign that read, "W's Report Card: death, destruction, debt, deficit, deceit," with each D highlighted in red.[222] Two hours before Bush's arrival, the protesters arrived to sing songs—Bruce Springsteen tunes playing loudly in the background—wave flags and give speeches. The road leading to the complex was also full of other protesters holding signs ranging from "Impeach the Murdering Liar" to "How many pints of blood are in a gallon of gas?" referring to the accusation the war in Iraq was fought over oil. Perhaps even for the president, the hardest display to miss was a long string from which fifty-four placards hung, each with the face, name and hometown of a New Jersey soldier who had died in the Iraq War.[223] The scene was a clear departure from just a decade earlier, when a supporter handed Bill Clinton a baby as he made his way through a cheering crowd. It was also far removed from when Teddy Roosevelt stopped the car to greet an old lady among the one-hundred-thousand-person crowd that welcomed him to New Jersey.

Upholding the protesters' constitutional rights, Edison mayor Jun Choi asked the city's police to escort the hecklers to an intersection where they could be noticed and heard by the presidential motorcade. In a comment unheard of in the past, especially when referring to a visit by a sitting president of the United States, the mayor said to the press, "I sure hope this is the last time President Bush comes to Edison." When asked to elaborate, Choi stated, "Our country is at a crossroads, and the real issues that really matter for working families, the backbone of our country…are not being addressed [by the president]." He finished his comments by calling Bush's foreign policy the worst in United States history. There certainly was not a lot of love for President Bush in New Jersey—and perhaps not all that much left for the presidency itself.

The partisan politics only got worse by the time Bush's successor, Barrack H. Obama's, *Marine One* helicopter touched down in the Garden State on October 31, 2012. The Democratic president was in town to see the devastation left behind by Hurricane Sandy, yet all the media could talk about was the "audacity" of New Jersey Republican governor Chris Christie budding up to him. It was fitting that the visit was a social media and internet spectacle that took away from the real intent of showing support for the severely damaged Jersey shore. Obama was truly the first president who embraced the growing social medium and technology, intertwining his presidency with social media. Shortly after his inauguration, the White House joined all the major social media outlets, including Facebook, iTunes, Twitter and Instagram. While the free exchange of information between the people and the most powerful man in America—and, for that matter, all politicians as a whole—was made easier than ever before, it left the door open for public ridicule as much as praise. For all the people who loved the image presented on social media, one of a fun, talented and cool leader, many fought back against his presidential policies. While it might be a stretch to say that the growth of social media led to the growing animosity or division among the American political spectrum, it would be equally dangerous to dismiss its role in abetting it.

President Obama battled a very oppositional Republican Party backed by a feverous supporter base throughout his two terms. His primary opponents viewed his policies of providing health coverage to all Americans through the Affordable Care Act and the $800 billion American Recovery and Reinvestment Act aimed at ending the 2008 recession as an overextension of the executive powers granted to him by the Constitution. And now, with social media platforms making the relationship between politicians and their constituents seem that much closer, people felt further removed from antiquated barriers of having to respect their leaders. One's once-private opinions discussed at the dinner table were now transcribed and sent to millions of like-minded people worldwide. The resulting division between people based on their political views took on a more personal connotation, further dividing the American people on issues they could once openly discuss.

President Barrack Obama visited New Jersey on October 31, 2012, two days after Hurricane Sandy made landfall in the state's southernmost region. The outspoken and brash New Jersey governor Chris Christie, who had already made a name for himself nationally as an up-and-coming force in the Republican Party, was on deck to meet the president and show him around the state. Christie, who would be reelected by a wide margin just a year later, only to finish his term as one of the least-popular governors in the nation following a political scandal, was seen at the time as the perfect

Governor Chris Christie and President Obama meeting with the evacuees of Hurricane Sandy on October 31, 2012. *Staff photographer: Kevin R. Wexler;* Herald News *(Passaic, NJ), November 1, 2012.*

counter to Obama. Yet to the dismay of many Republicans, the New Jersey governor placed partisan politics aside and graciously welcomed the American president to the Garden State, and the divisive media and social media had a tough time with it. Instead of treating the presidential visit as a somber occurrence, the news made it more about how out-of-character the state governor acted toward his opponent, not about bringing attention to the plight of those hurt by the terrible storm.

As the two men toured the Jersey shore, the media quickly pointed out their message of nonpartisan governing. After Obama arrived on *Air Force One*, Governor Christie greeted him, and the two were quickly back in the air, touring the area for one hour in the *Marine One* helicopter. Upon landing, a limousine took the president and governor to a nearby community center that had been turned into a shelter for displaced persons. The commander in chief, dressed informally in a simple jacket and slacks, circulated the room and greeted all who came near him, hugging, shaking hands and taking pictures with all who asked. After getting everyone's attention to highlight the amazing work of the cooks who served food for eighteen hours straight, the president received much cheer, even from those who did not necessarily vote for him in the last election. One woman who identified herself as a Republican stated that it was an honor to be in the same room as the American president. "It's nice that he thinks of the little people, too," she said.[224] The nonpartisan politics were not lost on those who were present during the visit. A woman who called herself a "die-hard" Democrat and "Obama supporter" praised the Republican governor Chris Christie: "I think he's been wonderful."[225] She then added, "He's sincere; I don't think he's being political right now." Speaking at the shelter, Obama further praised Christie: "Your governor is working overtime to make sure that as soon as possible, everybody can get back to normal."[226]

The Republican media was very quick to condemn Obama's state visit. The victims of Hurricane Sandy took a back seat to "Christie's warm embrace of Obama" at the visit's conclusion. What began with social media jokes about the supposed relationship between the two men quickly spiraled into GOP fury. When Republican Mitt Romney lost his election bid to the incumbent president a few days after the New Jersey visit, Rupert Murdoch, an influential news corporation chief, posted a Twitter message that said the governor's behavior in the Garden State might have been responsible for Obama's reelection.[227] Christie, seen at the time as the party's rising star, did spend a significant amount of time in the days after the visit praising the Democratic president's response in helping secure the right funding and

President Obama puts his hand on New Jersey governor Chris Christie during his visit to see the damage caused by Hurricane Sandy in 2012. New York Daily News, *October 31, 2012.*

assistance for New Jerseyans. The *New York Times* reported weeks later that Romney's out-of-state donors verbally attacked the New Jersey governor and his advisers, "demanding to know why he stood so close to the president on a tarmac" or "why he had boarded Mr. Obama's helicopter."[228] What should have been a nice gesture by an American president and showmanship of bipartisan politics from a welcoming state governor was turned into a social media spectacle, which showcased the deepening national divide. The media blamed Christie for skewing national election results. Also in doubt was his future role in the Republican Party, which, until then, saw him as a prospective presidential candidate.

President Obama's visit to New Jersey was a bit unconventional, as he was not there to speak to party supporters or present his party's platform. Yet the biggest takeaway from the stop was its highlight of the extent to which divisive politics of the twenty-first century played a role in diminishing the patriotic and celebratory spirit that once accompanied presidential visits across the nation. This new media-infused, they-versus-us political mentality would come into its own in 2016, when Donald J. Trump stunned the political world by winning the presidential election. The only American president without any former political or military experience, Trump defied norms and garnered the public's attention from the moment he took office. The president was always ready to stand up to a fight from across the political aisle, and he would use his position to openly criticize his opponents and perceived adversaries. No elected official—regardless of party affiliation—or foreign head of state was ever safe from the twenty-six thousand tweets Trump posted as president.[229] Twitter would eventually suspend the commander in chief's account after it deemed some of his messages were provocative.

According to the Pew Research Center, over his four years as president, Trump's "outspoken nature and his willingness to upend past customs and expectations of presidential behavior made him a constant focus of public attention, as well as a source of deep partisan divisions."[230] And as much as social media ridiculed the president's hyperpatriotic rallies and spread the resentment of his policies, it also did much to bring his supporters together. It is a commonly accepted belief that human beings do not like having their beliefs challenged. With the advent of social media and news networks catering to specific political affiliations, Trump supporters and dissenters would only follow specific online threads, watch certain news networks and listen to specific radio programs, shielding themselves from opposing viewpoints. This media-driven dichotomy partially led to the unprecedented political division between the two major political parties, something that was only further fueled by the president's "in your face" personality. In fact, according to the statistics, Trump divided the Republicans and Democrats more than any other chief executive going back three decades. An average of 86 percent of Republicans approved of Trump's handling of his job, compared with an average of just 6 percent of Democrats—the widest gap in approval of any president in the modern era of polling.[231] Still, those who loved Trump loved him. Trump rallies were a sight to behold. American flags, "Make America Great Again" hats and Trump signs blanked the crowds of thousands. The fervor was the closest to that of presidential visits of the early twentieth century as it could get.

An analysis following Trump's presidency conducted by the *Atlantic* pointed out that to the president's supporters, who saw themselves surrounded by liberal-leaning media, the crowd sizes at the Trump rallies provided them with a certain level of validity. In their own way, "it was proof that they [were] part of the American majority."[232] It was because of all of this that it was a big deal when President Trump finally chose to hold one of his famous rallies in the Garden State, and this is also why one of the biggest points of his speech was him pointing out the size of the crowd that came out to see him.

The January 28, 2020 Trump Rally in Wildwood brought back many memories of past presidential visits, when thousands of people turned out to see their commander in chief. Although the forty-fifth president had owned property and frequented the Garden State previously, this was his first and only official rally held in the Democratically controlled New Jersey. His appearance also happened to take place merely hours after his attorneys finished presenting their defense against Trump's first impeachment trial (the

A HISTORY

Official White House portrait of President Donald J. Trump. *Library of Congress.*

controversial politician would become the only American president to be impeached twice during his term). As if the perceived hate and ridicule stemming from the left was not overwhelming enough for the former media personality, President Trump had found himself brought up on impeachment charges for allegedly soliciting foreign interference in the upcoming 2020 presidential election. Still, none of that stopped the New Jerseyans residing in the southernmost portion of the state from coming out in droves to see their commander in chief.

Even though the rally took place in the off season, with a majority of all restaurants and business closed for the winter, the parking lots and the boardwalk near the Wildwood Convention Center were packed. With news channels having direct camera feeds into the seaside town, anyone with an internet connection could have tapped in to see the thousands of Trump supporters lined up to catch a glimpse of the president. The rally was a first-come, first-served event, and many of those who showed up were not admitted to the already packed 7,500-seat arena. In all, a reported 100,000 people requested tickets to the rally.[233] Those who did not make it inside waited out in the cold weather and were surrounded by countless vendors selling "Make America Great Again" hats and T-shirts and even a stuffed animal known as a "Trumpy bear." Inside, the American president spoke for just over an hour, touching on everything from his recent impeachment trial to fake news, immigration and New Jersey's strong economy. Calling New Jerseyans "tough, smart and great people," Trump also singled out former governor Chris Christie for having done an excellent job with the state years prior, and Christie then sat proudly, watching the speech from the front row. Going on the defensive, the president admitted that the "fake media" would probably not report on the massive numbers of people who came to see him. He then claimed he was asked to move the rally to the Meadowlands MetLife Football Stadium but that he refused and instead preferred Wildwood's more "intimate" setting.[234] As Trump was giving his concluding remarks about the failure of the Democratic Party, his supporters who were waiting outside were locked in a loud yelling match with hundreds of anti-Trump protesters. A few decades earlier, this scene would be limited to a few opponents quietly holding dissenting signs away from newspaper journalists.

The last president to visit New Jersey before 2022 was Trump's Democratic successor, Joe Biden. Like Obama, under whom Biden served as vice president, Biden came to the Garden States to survey the damage caused by a natural disaster. Hurricane Ida struck the Jersey coast in September 2021, causing massive flooding and subsequent damage to many southern Jersey towns and cities. Nearly fifty people were killed across six states as Ida brought record rainfall to the Northern Seaboard, overwhelming rivers and sewer system, including the Garden State's Raritan River near Manville. Many individuals became trapped in the quickly rising waters, unable to leave their basements or cars as the weather only intensified into forming tornadoes. President Biden chose to come to New Jersey, as it was the Garden State where almost half (twenty-seven) of all the deaths occurred.[235] Walking the streets of the Lost Valley neighborhood of Manville with Democratic state senator Cory Booker and Democratic governor Philip Murphy, the president, wearing a mask due to the ongoing COVID pandemic, stopped to speak to adults and children alike. At one point, a woman wearing a "Make America Great Again" hat yelled in Biden's direction, calling him a "tyrant."[236]

Following Hurricane Katrina, which devastated New Orleans in 2005, presidents saw national crises as a way to showcase their empathy toward the American people. It was a poignant lesson learned in the aftermath of Katrina. The media accused President George W. Bush of being aloof from the tragedy, waiting two full days after the worst days of the storm to cut his vacation short and come back to Washington, D.C. When the White House released pictures of the president surveying the devastation from the window of *Air Force One* while flying over Louisiana, the accusations of detachment and uncaring only intensified. Obama did not make the same mistake with Hurricane Sandy in 2012, nor did Biden in 2020. And while Obama made the visit to the Garden State work for him—at least according to the Republican press—securing votes in the upcoming election, Biden also saw his stop in New Jersey as a perfect way to endorse his policies. After calling for federal spending to strengthen the infrastructure to better defend New Jerseyans and their property from future storms, Biden lumped the disaster in with wildfires, tornadoes and other extreme weather caused by "climate change."[237] At the time of the president's visit, his proposed national infrastructure plan worth $1 trillion was pending in Congress. In the upcoming days, he would add $24 billion to his proposal to cover the costs of Hurricane Ida and other national disasters.[238] His brief thirty-minute stop in New Jersey become a perfect backdrop for his party's political agenda.

The last meaningful presidential visit to New Jersey, albeit unintentional, reminded us of most of the visits that came before it. The famous economist Thomas Sowell once said, "No one really understands politics until they understand that politicians are not trying to solve our problems. They are trying to solve their own problems—of which, getting elected and reelected are no. 1 and no. 2. Whatever is no. 3 is far behind."

AFTERWORD

Writing a book about politicians and political events was quite a task, especially when trying not to make the book seem too political. From the onset, my task was to simply retell stories of meaningful presidential visits to my home state of New Jersey. As mentioned in the introduction, it would have been impossible to relate a complete account of every single visit to the state by the incumbent—or even past—American president. While making my selection, I tried to look at the times when the said stop in the Garden State was meaningful or had some historical significance. I tried to place each story and visit within the greater historical context. And while I did not want the book to concentrate strictly on a president's stomping through the state in an election or reelection year, some of those visits were the most important.

It was not my intent to judge the policies of any of the leaders mentioned in these pages; rather, I wanted to provide a narrative that stuck strictly to the facts, at least as they were reported at the time. Much of what I wrote about came from old newspapers and memoirs collected by various historical societies. The local newspapers proved invaluable to this research. Where applicable, their political bias based on the state's region was acknowledged and countered with the opposite view.

In his monumental work *What Is History?*, historian Edward Hallett Carr spent a significant amount of time and research outlining the historians' bias and moral judgments. Based on his assertions, all of history is fundamentally flawed. Individual bias begins with the person recording in their mind the event they are experiencing and then interpreting it for themselves. Whether it is a person seeing the event firsthand or someone who reads about it later, the real facts of what had happened are continuously interpreted and reinterpreted and thus skewed, as the memory itself is already interpreted the first time it is collected. It begs the question: is there such a thing as pure, unbiased history? In the truest sense, the answer is no. Yet, Carr admitted, although each historian collecting their facts needs to know that even in their purest form, they are only interpretations of the real events and that these will then once again be interpreted by the historian collecting them, albeit unintentionally, it is still the historian's job to strive to present the most unbiased narrative possible. I set out to conduct my research and write this book with this very thought in mind. I can only hope that, to some extent, I succeeded.

NOTES

Preface

1. Dallek, *Hail to the Chief*, xi.
2. Gil Troy, "The Surprisingly Glamorous History of New Jersey Presidential Vacations," *Daily Beast*, https://www.thedailybeast.com/when-new-jersey-was-the-vacation-of-choice-for-presidents.

Chapter 1

3. Alexander Stephens, a speech delivered before the Georgia House of Representatives, November 14, 1860, https://civilwarcauses.org/steph2.htm.
4. Cunningham and Hill, *America's Main Road*, 173.
5. Hull, *Mirror on America*, 176.
6. Cunningham and Hill, *America's Main Road*, 175.
7. New Jersey Department of State, "Lincoln and New Jersey," https://www.nj.gov/state/archives/lincoln.html#electoral.
8. Hull, *Mirror on America*, 177.
9. "The President Elect: Full Details of the Journey from New York to Philadelphia," *Holmes County Republican* (Millersburg, OH), February 28, 1861, 1.
10. Ibid.
11. Ibid.

12. Earl Schenck Miers, *New Jersey and the Civil War*, New Jersey Historical Series (Princeton, NJ: D. Van Nostrand Company Inc., 1964), 8.
13. Hull, *Mirror on America*, 178.
14. Ibid., 179.
15. Ibid., 188.
16. Ibid., 194.

Chapter 2

17. Wilson, *Jersey Shore*, 70.
18. Troy, "Surprisingly Glamorous History."
19. Ibid.
20. Wilson, *Jersey Shore*, 72.
21. Karen Fox, "The Halls Presidents Walked," Cape May History, https://www.capemay.com/blog/2012/02/the-halls-presidents-walked/.
22. Ibid.
23. Ibid.
24. Wilson, *Jersey Shore*, 73.
25. Ibid.
26. Ibid., 77.
27. Fleming, *History*, 138.
28. Ibid., 139.
29. Wilson, *Jersey Shore*, 75.
30. Fleming, *History*, 140.
31. Ibid., 141.
32. Fox, "Halls Presidents Walked."
33. Ibid.
34. Wilson, *Jersey Shore*, 73.

Chapter 3

35. Morgan, *Our Presidents*, 204.
36. "A Shot That Will Startle the Entire World," *Memphis* (TN) *Daily Appeal*, July 3, 1881, 1.
37. Ibid.
38. Candice Millard, *Destiny of the Republic: A Tale of Madness, Medicine, and the Murder or a President* (New York: Anchor Books, 2011), 167.

39. Ibid., 168.

40. Mappen, *Jerseyana*, 94.

41. Asbury Park Press, "Weird NJ: Presidential Death on the Jersey Shore," https://www.app.com/story/news/local/eatontown-asbury-park/long-branch/2014/11/23/weird-nj-presidential-death-jersey-shore/19440133/.

42. "The President: Preparing for the Journey to Long Branch To-Day," *Morning Post* (Camden, NJ), September 6, 1881, 1.

43. Ibid.

44. Millard, *Destiny of the Republic*, 261.

45. Ibid.

46. Fred Rosen, *Murdering the President: Alexander Graham Bell and the Race to Save James Garfield* (Lincoln: University of Nebraska Press, 2016), 171.

47. Millard, *Destiny of the Republic*, 263.

48. Mappen, *Jerseyana*, 94.

49. Rosen, *Murdering the President*, 173.

50. Mappen, *Jerseyana*, 96.

51. Fleming, *History*, 142.

52. Ibid.

53. Erik Larsen, "A Sitting American President Dies in Long Branch," Asbury Park Press, September 19, 2017, https://www.app.com/story/news/history/erik-larsen/2017/09/19/sitting-american-president-dies-long-branch/667661001/.

Chapter 4

54. Boller, *Presidential Campaigns*, 192.

55. G. Scott Thomas, *Counting the Votes: A New Way to Analyze America's Presidential Elections* (Westport, CT: Praeger, 2015), 160.

56. Boller, *Presidential Campaigns*, 197.

57. Cunningham and Hill, *America's Main Road*, 261.

58. Ibid., 263.

59. Hull, *Mirror on America*, 266.

60. "Three Presidential Candidates Whirl Through Jersey," *Long Branch* (NJ) *Daily Record*, May 24, 1912, 1.

61. "Thousands Honored Nation's Chief Upon His First Visit to Camden Last Night," *Camden* (NJ) *Daily Courier*, May 24, 1912, 1.

62. Ibid.

63. Ibid.

64. "Thousands Greet Taft," *Morning Call* (Paterson, NJ), May 24, 1912, 9.

65. "President Taft at the Armory Tonight," *Evening Record* (Hackensack, NJ), May 25, 1912, 1.

66. "President Taft's Visit Aroused Entire City," *Morning Call* (Paterson, NJ), May 27, 1912, 1.

67. Ibid., 9.

68. "10,000 Heard Mr. Roosevelt Speak," *Morning Call* (Paterson, NJ), May 24, 1912, 1.

69. "Thousands Hereabout Greet 'Teddy,'" *Passaic* (NJ) *Daily News*, May 24, 1912, 7.

70. Ibid.

71. Ibid.

72. "10,000 Heard," *Morning Call* (Paterson, NJ), 1.

73. Ibid.

74. "Roosevelt on Visit to Bergen County Towns," *Evening Record* (Hackensack, NJ), May 24, 1912.

75. Ibid.

76. "Letter from Asbury Park Press Editor," *Asbury Park* (NJ) *Press*, May 25, 1912, 6.

77. Ibid.

78. "Wilson Meeting Will Close Strenuous Campaign," *Passaic* (NJ) *Daily Herald*, November 2, 1912, 1.

79. "Governor Wilson Receives Warm Monmouth Greeting; Praises Scully and Taylor," *Long Branch* (NJ) *Daily Record*, November 4, 1912, 6.

80. "Governor Recovering from Scalp Wound," *Long Branch* (NJ) *Daily Record*, November 4, 1912, 6.

81. Cunningham and Hill, *America's Main Road*, 264.

Chapter 5

82. Boller, *Presidential Campaigns*, 240.

83. Hull, *Mirror on America*, 300.

84. Ibid., 301.

85. Ibid., 304.

86. Arthur Guarino, "New Jersey in the Great Depression," *Garden State Legacy*, no. 24 (June 2014), https://gardenstatelegacy.com/files/Time_of_Despair_Time_of_Hope_Guarino_GSL24.pdf.

87. Hull, *Mirror on America*, 304.

88. Cunningham and Hill, *America's Main Road*, 291–92.

89. Hull, *Mirror on America*, 306.

90. Walter LaFaber, *The American Century, A History of the United States Since the 1890s* (New York: Routledge Press, 2008), 171.

91. Bob Ingle, *The Soprano State: New Jersey's Culture of Corruption* (New York: St. Martin's Press, 2008), 74.

92. Willard Edwards, "$10,000 Show Is Given in Jersey for Roosevelt," *Chicago Daily Tribune*, October 3, 1936, 10.

93. Philip Pearl, "Roosevelt on 'Personal Appearance' Swing," *San Francisco Examiner*, October 3, 1936, 7.

94. Edwards, "Show Is Given in Jersey," 10.

95. History Central, "1932 Election Results Hoover vs. Roosevelt," https://www.historycentral.com/elections/1932.html.

96. "Landon Favors U.S. Laws for Protection of Labor; President Speaks in Bayonne," *Daily Home News* (New Brunswick, NJ), October 28, 1936, 1.

97. Ibid., 12.

98. Ibid.

99. "100,000 Cheer F.R. in Record Ovation Here," *Evening Courier* (Camden, NJ), October 30, 1936, 1.

100. Ibid.

101. Ibid.

102. Ibid.

103. Ibid.

104. Alan Brinkley, *American History* (Orlando, FL: Houghton Mifflin Harcourt Publishing, 2018), 813.

105. Hull, *Mirror on America*, 309.

Chapter 6

106. "Eisenhower Invades North New Jersey," *Plainfield Courier News* (Bridgewater, NJ), October 16, 1952, 1.

107. Parmet, *Eisenhower*, 7.

108. George Brown Tindall, *America: A Narrative History*, 3rd ed. (New York: W.W. Norton & Company, 1992), 1,294.

109. Boller, *Presidential Campaigns*, 285.

110. Ibid., 282.

111. Ibid.

112. Ibid.

113. "Eisenhower Invades," *Plainfield Courier News*, 1.

114. "Ike Says Demos Are Indicted by Clean-Up Failure," *Knoxville* (TN) *News Sentinel*, October 17, 1952, 2.

115. "Eisenhower's Appearance Draws Thousands to City," *Daily Home News* (New Brunswick, NJ), October 17, 1952, 1.

116. Ibid., 2.

117. Frank M. Deiner, "Ike Tells Voters to Demand Government They Can Respect," *Daily Home News* (New Brunswick, NJ), October 18, 1952, 1.

118. Elihu Joseph, "General Was Late, But Crowd Stayed to Cheer Him Lustily," *Daily Home News* (New Brunswick, NJ), October 18, 1952, 1.

119. Deiner, "Demand Government They Can Respect," 2.

120. Ibid., 1.

121. "Ike Says He's Still No Deal Candidate," *Port Huron* (MI) *Times*, October 18, 1952, 1.

122. James P. Hackett, "Republicans See Tremendous Vote as Result of Ike's Tour of State," *Bergen Evening Record* (Hackensack, NJ), October 18, 1952, 1.

123. "Washington with Thomas Stokes," *Charlotte* (NC) *Observer*, October 8, 1948, 18A.

124. Joseph S. Wells, "Country Is More Prosperous, President Declares in Camden," *Courier Post* (Camden, NJ), October 22, 1952, 10.

125. Ibid.

126. Osmonde Spaar, "Truman's Crowds Amazing," *Herald News* (Passaic, NJ), October 22, 1952, 1.

127. Ibid.

128. Ibid., 2.

129. Wells, "Country Is More Prosperous," 10.

130. Spaar, "Truman's Crowds Amazing," 2.

131. "Harry Gets into the Act," *Daily Home News* (New Brunswick, NJ), September 2, 1961, 9.

132. Hackett, "Republicans See Tremendous Vote," 2.

Chapter 7

133. Robert H. Resnick, "Kennedy Stumps Jersey in Bid for Every Vote," *Vineland* (NJ) *Times Journal*, November 7, 1960, 11.

134. "Cheering Bergen, Hudson, Essex Crowds Greet JFK," *Paterson* (NJ) *Evening News*, November 7, 1960, 50.
135. Ibid.
136. Ibid.
137. Ibid.
138. Boller, *Presidential Campaigns*, 312.
139. Ibid.
140. Ibid.
141. Ibid., 314.
142. Bernard Silverstein, "Airport Fence Saves President from Being Overrun by Enthusiastic Crowd," *Paterson* (NJ) *News*, October 15, 1964, 10.
143. Ibid.
144. Ibid.
145. Joseph Quartucci, "It Wasn't Beatlemania at Mall, It Was Johnsonmania," *Paterson* (NJ) *News*, October 15, 1964, 10.
146. Ibid.
147. Ibid.
148. Ibid.
149. "CORE Unit Adds Grim Note to LBJ Bergen Rally," *Herald News* (Passaic, NJ), October 15, 1964, 2.
150. Robert Comstock, "Democrat Hopes Up After Visit," *Morning Call* (Paterson, NJ), October 15, 1964, 8.
151. Quartucci, "It Wasn't Beatlemania," 10.
152. Comstock, "Democrat Hopes Up," 8.
153. Fleming, *History*, 196.
154. Hull, *Mirror on America*, 344.

Chapter 8

155. Boller, *Presidential Campaigns*, 372.
156. Frank Newport, "Ronald Reagan from the People's Perspective: A Gallup Poll Review," Gallup, https://news.gallup.com/poll/11887/ronald-reagan-from-peoples-perspective-gallup-poll-review.aspx.
157. Eric Foner, *Give Me Liberty: An American History*, 2nd ed. (New York: W.W. Norton, 2009), 987.
158. W.J. Rorabaugh, *America! A Concise History* (Belmont, CA: Wadsworth Publishing, 1993), 608.

159. Reagan Foundation, "Reagan the Man," https://www. reaganfoundation.org/ronald-reagan/the-presidency/reagan-the-man/.
160. Ibid.
161. Boller, *Presidential Campaigns*, 370.
162. Ibid., 371.
163. "New Jersey Primary Heating Up," *Daily Record* (Morristown, NJ), May 20, 1984, 4.
164. Elissa McCrary, "New Jersey Battleground: State Regarded as Key to Presidential Victory," *Asbury Park* (NJ) *Press*, July 27, 1984, 23.
165. Ibid.
166. Ibid.
167. Ibid.
168. "Reagan Praises Jersey Effort to Halt Drunk Driving," *Daily Register* (Red Bank, NJ), June 21, 1984, 1.
169. Lee Keough, "A Moment of Sadness Amid the Joy," *Herald News* (Passaic, NJ), June 21, 1984, 1.
170. "Reagan Praises Jersey Effort," *Daily Register* (Red Bank, NJ), 1.
171. Keough, "Moment of Sadness," 1.
172. Brad Rudin, "Students Pleased by Reagan Visit," *Herald News* (Passaic, NJ), June 21, 1984, 7.
173. Ibid.
174. Tom Hester, "President Woos N.J.'s 'Heartland,'" *Home News* (New Brunswick, NJ), July 27, 1884, 1.
175. Ibid.
176. Ibid.
177. Michael J. Kelly, "Elizabeth Warms Up to President," *Courier News* (Bridgewater, NJ), July 27, 1984, 3.
178. Hester, "President Woos," 1.
179. Ibid.
180. Ibid.
181. "Debate Parties Add to the Democrats' Coffers," *Asbury Park* (NJ) *Press*, October 9, 1984, 8.
182. Leslie Werstein, "Cheers, Drizzle Greet Regan in Jersey Visit," *Courier News* (Bridgewater, NJ), October 27, 1984, 1.
183. Ibid.
184. Edward J. Mullin, "Hackensack Gives Reagan Big Welcome," *Herald News* (Passaic, NJ), October 27, 1984, 4.
185. Ibid.
186. Werstein, "Cheers, Drizzle Greet Regan," 3.

187. Ibid.

188. Dale Russakoff, "Election '84 Issue: The Environment," *Washington Post*, October 14, 1984, https://www.washingtonpost.com/archive/politics/1984/10/14/election-84-issue-the-environment/64724163-624d-4cb1-a0f2-8a90ccf73778/.

189. Ibid.

190. Ibid.

191. Ibid.

192. Department of State, New Jersey Division of Elections, "Election Information and Results Archive: 1984 Election Results," https://nj.gov/state/elections/election-information-1984.shtml#general.

193. Ibid.

194. Boller, *Presidential Campaigns*, 373.

Chapter 9

195. Adam Nagourney, "Clinton Speaks to the MTV Generation," *San Bernardo* (CA) *County Sun*, June 17, 1992, 1.

196. Rorabaugh, *America!*, 622.

197. Molly Omstead, "The *New York Times* Reported George H.W. Bush Was Infamously Out of Touch at Supermarket in 1992, But the Gaffe Probably Never Happened," Insider, December 3, 2018, https://www.businessinsider.com/george-hw-bush-out-of-touch-gaffe-probably-didnt-happen-2018-12.

198. Rorabaugh, *America!*, 624.

199. Douglas Brinkley, "Bill Clinton Wins the White House," in *America's Decades: 1990s*, edited by Stuart A. Kallen (San Diego, CA: Greenhaven Press Inc., 2000), 16.

200. Inside Jersey, "When Jersey Mattered in the Presidential Race," https://www.nj.com/inside-jersey/2012/10/when_jersey_mattered_in_the_presidential_race.html.

201. "Surge of New Voters Is Heaviest Since '84," *Courier News* (Bridgewater, NJ), October 27, 1992, 4.

202. Inside Jersey, "When Jersey Mattered."

203. Pat Politano, "Bush Must Work for Votes Here; Experts," *Courier News* (Bridgewater, NJ), July 27, 1992, 2.

204. Steve Marlowe, "Bush Wows Bergen," *Herald & News* (Passaic, NJ), July 22, 1992, 8.

205. Ibid.

206. Pasquale DiFulco, "Presidential Visit Fails to Inspire City's Critics," *Herald & News* (Passaic, NJ), July 22, 1992, 8.

207. Terry Mutchler, "Bill and Al's Excellent Adventure Begins," *Daily Record* (Morristown, NJ), July 18, 1992, 2.

208. Colleen O'Dea, "Clinton Plugs Health Plan," *Daily Record* (Morristown, NJ), September 25, 1992, 1.

209. "Clinton Accepts Comeuppance," *Record* (Hackensack, NJ), September 25, 1992, 12.

210. Christopher Hann, "Bush Repeats Challenge at Newark Union," *Courier News* (Bridgewater, NJ), October 1, 1992, 1.

211. Audrey Kelly, "Dem Challenger Offers to Join President on TV," *Central New Jersey Home News* (New Brunswick, NJ), October 1, 1992, 1.

212. Colleen O'Dea, "Kean Away as Clinton Makes Stop at Drew," *Daily Record* (Morristown, NJ), October 1, 1992, 1.

213. Ibid.

214. Ibid.

215. Pat Politano, "Bush Visits Edison," *Courier News* (Bridgewater, NJ), October 17, 1992, 1.

216. Jane E. Allen, "Stars Come out for Clinton," *Courier Post* (Camden, NJ), November 2, 1992, 1.

217. Colleen Mancino, "Students Across the State 'Elect' Clinton President," *Record* (Hackensack, NJ), October 30, 1992, 15.

Chapter 10

218. Paulina Cachero, "U.S. Taxpayers Have Reportedly Paid an Average of $8,000 Each and Over $2 Trillion Total for the Iraq War Alone," Business Insider, https://www.businessinsider.com/us-taxpayers-spent-8000-each-2-trillion-iraq-war-study-2020-2.

219. Erica Harbatkin, "Terrorism, Taxes Dominate Speech at GOP Fundraiser," *Daily Record* (Morristown, NJ), May 31, 2007, A6.

220. Ibid.

221. Ibid.

222. Gene Racz and John Majeski, "Bush Opponents Jeer His Arrival in Edison," *Daily Record* (Morristown, NJ), May 31, 2007, A6.

223. Ibid.

224. Karen Sudol, "Obama Vows Help Until N.J. Is Rebuilt," *Herald News* (Passaic, NJ), November 1, 2012, 7.

225. Anthony Campisi, "Obama, Christie Provide Reassurance," *Herald News* (Passaic, NJ), November 1, 2012, 7.

226. Sudol, "Obama Vows Help," 7.

227. Michael Barbaro, "After Obama, Christie Wants a G.O.P. Hug," *New York Times*, https://www.nytimes.com/2012/11/20/us/politics/after-embrace-of-obama-chris-christie-woos-a-wary-gop.html.

228. Ibid.

229. Michael Dimock, "How America Changed During Donald Trump's Presidency," Pew Research Center, https://www.pewresearch.org/2021/01/29/how-america-changed-during-donald-trumps-presidency/.

230. Ibid.

231. Ibid.

232. Elaine Godfrey, "Trump Fans Have Found Their Safe Space," *Atlantic*, https://www.theatlantic.com/politics/archive/2022/01/trump-rally-bubble-crowd-size/621292/.

233. Brianna Kudisch, "Wildwood Live Webcams Show Scenes at Trump's Rally at the Jersey Shore," NJ.com, https://www.nj.com/cape-may-county/2020/01/wildwood-live-webcams-show-crowds-at-trumps-rally-at-the-jersey-shore.html.

234. Jonathan D. Salant, "Donald Trump Just Held a Loud (and Packed) Rally in Wildwood. 'I Love New Jersey,' He Declared," NJ.com, https://www.nj.com/politics/2020/01/donald-trump-holds-raucous-rally-in-wildwood.html.

235. Aamer Madhani, "Biden Surveys New Jersey Storm Damage After Deadly Flooding," WHYY, https://whyy.org/articles/biden-to-survey-ny-and-nj-storm-damage-after-deadly-flooding/.

236. Ibid.

237. Ibid.

238. Ibid.

SELECTED BIBLIOGRAPHY

Books

Bailey, Thomas Andrew. *A Diplomatic History of the American People*. Englewood, NJ: Prentice-Hall, 1990.

Beschloss, Michael R. *Presidential Courage: Brave Leaders and How They Changed America, 1789–1989*. New York: Simon and Schuster, 2008.

Boller, Paul F. *Presidential Campaigns: From George Washington to George W. Bush*. New York: Oxford University Press, 2010.

Brands, H.W. *Reagan: The Life*. New York: Anchor Books, 2016.

Burns, James MacGregor, and Susan Dunn. *The Three Roosevelts: A Biography of the Family That Transformed America*. New York: Atlantic, 2001.

Caro, Robert A. *The Years of Lyndon Johnson*. New York: Knopf, 2013.

Clinton, Bill. *My Life: Bill Clinton*. New York: Random House Inc., 2004.

Cooper, John Milton. *Pivotal Decades: The United States, 1900–1920*. New York: Norton, 1990.

Cunningham, John T. *This Is New Jersey*. New Brunswick, NJ: Rutgers University Press, 1994.

Cunningham, John T., and Homer Hill. *New Jersey: America's Main Road*. Garden City, NY: Doubleday, 1976.

Dallek, Robert. *Hail to the Chief: The Making and Unmaking of American Presidents*. New York: Oxford University Press, 2001.

Dorer, Harry, and John T. Cunningham. *This Was New Jersey: As Seen by Photographer Harry C. Dorer*. New Brunswick, NJ: Rivergate Books, 2007.

Fleming, Thomas J. *New Jersey: A History*. New York: Norton, 1984.

Hull, Joan C. *Teacher's Guide for New Jersey: A Mirror on America*. Florham Park, NJ: Afton, 1978.

Mappen, Marc. *Jerseyana: The Underside of New Jersey History*. New Brunswick, NJ: Rutgers University Press, 1992.

McCullough, David G. *Mornings on Horseback*. New York: Touchstone, 1981.

————. *Truman*. New York: Simon and Schuster, 1992.

Meacham, Jon. *Destiny and Power: The American Odyssey of George Herbert Walker Bush*. New York: Random House, 2016.

Morgan, James. *Our Presidents*. New York: Collier-Macmillan, 1969.

Parmet, Herbert S. *Eisenhower & the American Crusades: With a New Introduction by the Author, Herbert S. Parmet*. New Brunswick, NJ: Transaction Publishing, 1998.

Studley, Miriam Van Arsdale. *Historic New Jersey Through Visitors' Eyes*. Princeton, NJ: D. Van Nostrand Company Inc., 1964.

Taft, William H., and David Henry Burton. *William Howard Taft: Essential Writings and Addresses*. Madison, NJ: Fairleigh Dickinson University Press, 2009.

Vecoli, Rudolph J. *People of New Jersey*. Princeton, NJ: Van Nostrand, 1965.

Whitney, David C., and Robin Vaughn Whitney. *The American Presidents*. Pleasantville, NY: Reader's Digest Association, 2012.

Wilson, Harold Fisher. *The Story of the Jersey Shore*. Princeton, NJ: D. Van Nostrand Company Inc., 1964.

New Jersey Historic Newspapers

Asbury Park Press (Asbury Park)

Bergen Evening Record (Hackensack)

Camden Daily Courier (Camden)

Daily Home News (Bayonne)

Daily Home News (New Brunswick)

Daily News (Morristown)

Evening Courier (Camden)

Evening Record (Hackensack)

Herald News (Passaic)

Long Branch Daily Record (Long Branch)

Morning Call (Paterson)

Morning Post (Camden)

Passaic Daily Herald (Passaic)

Passaic Daily News (Passaic)

Paterson Evening News (Paterson)

Plainfield Courier News (Bridgewater)

Vineland Times Journal (Vineland)

ABOUT THE AUTHOR

Peter Zablocki is a historian, educator and author of numerous books detailing New Jersey's history. His articles often appear in various popular history publications, and his podcast, *History Teachers Talking*, is available on all popular streaming platforms. For more information about his books, podcast or any upcoming events, visit www.peterzablocki.com.

Visit us at
www.historypress.com
···